7/8284

Homosexuality and Literature 1890-1930

By the same author

Fiction and the Colonial Experience
The Wounded Spirit: A Study of 'Seven Pillars of Wisdom'
T. E. Lawrence: A Bibliography
Painting and the Novel
A Reader's Guide to George Orwell
George Orwell: The Critical Heritage
George Orwell: An Annotated Bibliography of Criticism
A Catalogue of the Library of Siegfried Sassoon
A Fever at the Core: The Idealist in Politics
Married to Genius

Homosexuality and Literature 1890-1930

JEFFREY MEYERS

University of London
THE ATHLONE PRESS
1977

Published by
THE ATHLONE PRESS
UNIVERSITY OF LONDON
at 4 Gower Street London WC1

Distributed by Tiptree Book Services Ltd
Tiptree, Essex

© *Jeffrey Meyers* 1977

ISBN 0 485 11168 3

Printed in Great Britain by
T. & A. CONSTABLE LTD
EDINBURGH

Para
Felipe y Concha
Días en Benalmádena

ACKNOWLEDGMENTS

Parts of this book have appeared in the *London Magazine, Southern Review* and *English Literature in Transition*, and I am grateful to the editors for permission to reprint.

J. M.

CONTENTS

I

Introduction

> From my most unnoticed actions
> and my most veiled writing —
> from these alone will I be understood.
>   C. P. Cavafy, 'Hidden Things'

I

When I originally discussed the idea of this book with a professor of English, he remarked that it was really quite difficult to find any serious author in the last seventy years who was not involved with homosexuality in one way or another. But though a great deal has been written, for example, about the Bloomsbury Group, there has been very little discussion of how homosexuality, which helped to form their ethos, was manifested in their art. *Homosexuality and Literature* seeks to explore an important theme in modern European literature, to add a new dimension of interest to the works discussed by clarifying aspects that are often missed or ignored, and to illuminate the character and creative process of their authors by analysing the sexual problems that were sublimated and transcended in their art.

The clandestine predilections of homosexual novelists are both an obstacle and a stimulus to art, and lead to a creative tension between repression and expression. The novels become a raid on inarticulate feelings, and force the authors to find a language of reticence and evasion, obliqueness and indirection, to convey their theme. Homosexual novels are characteristically subtle, allusive and symbolic — the very qualities we now admire in the poetry of Yeats and Eliot, and the novels of Flaubert and Henry James — and form an eighth kind of literary ambiguity. For the ambiguous expression of the repressed, the hidden and the sometimes secret theme suggests a moral ambiguity as well. If a specifically homosexual tone, sensibility, vision or mode of apprehension exists, then it would be characterized by these cautious and covert qualities, and by the use of art to conceal rather than to reveal the actual theme of the novel: 'Il n'y a de vérité que dans les nuances'.

In *The Picture of Dorian Gray* the inward corruption of Wilde's hero is frequently hinted at but not defined, and we never discover what Dorian has actually done because his crime cannot be expressed. Michel, in Gide's *The Immoralist,* is forced to dissimulate about the secret side of his life until a series of homosexual temptations lead him to the discovery of his true nature. The homosexual theme of Mann's *Death in Venice* is overt but symbolic: both a manifestation of strain and disorder and of an artist's exalted but tragic search for perfection. In contrast to the covert expression of Wilde and Gide, and the symbolism of Mann, Musil realistically portrays the sado-masochistic aspects of inversion.

Like Wilde and Gide, Proust had to devise a strategy that would allow him to portray inverts in *Cities of the Plain* without sacrificing the sympathy of his readers, and he frequently represents homosexual love in a heterosexual disguise. In Conrad too there is a vital tension between the conventional and subterranean themes, and *Victory* is actually a compromise between Conrad's desire to write openly about homosexuality and his need to suppress the sexual core of his novel. *A Room With A View* and *Maurice* present an interesting contrast between Forster's subtle concealment in the book published in his lifetime and his didactic failure in the posthumous work.

In his spiritual autobiography, *Seven Pillars of Wisdom,* T. E. Lawrence was unable to write the clear truth about himself and was forced to portray his torture and rape at Deraa in an oblique and metaphorical manner. And in four major novels D. H. Lawrence considers homosexuality as a more meaningful and transcendent alternative to heterosexual love, but also portrays the scenes of male friendship in a rhythmic, incantatory, ambiguous and poetic language that obscures yet intensifies his real theme.

The problem of the writer who publicly expresses private feelings and, by implication, acts that are both taboo and sensational, is matched by the problem of the critic who must find appropriate words to describe and analyse homosexual art. I have no desire to praise or condemn homosexuality; and do not imply a moral judgment when I use words like invert, pederast and perverse, which have negative connotations. I do hope, however, to maintain the sympathetic attitude that is necessary to understand any work of art.

Because of the large number of homosexual writers — as well as authors like Mann, Musil, D. H. Lawrence and Conrad who dealt with homosexual themes — it was necessary to be selective[1]. I have therefore chosen both difficult and significant works which were written between 1890 and 1930 when this theme achieves its finest literary expression, which treat the complex theme in various ways and lend themselves to intensive analysis from this point of view, and which are related to each other and form a natural pattern and progression. I felt it would be more valuable and interesting to concentrate on a small number of great works than to write a general survey of novels about and by homosexuals[2]. I have not considered lesbian novels like Vernon Lee's *Miss Brown* (1884), Colette's *Claudine en ménage* (1902), Gertrude Stein's *Q.E.D.* (1903, first published in 1950 as *Things As They Are*), Vita Sackville-West's *Challenge* (1924), Olive Schreiner's unfinished *From Man to Man* (1926) and Radclyffe Hall's didactic *The Well of Loneliness* (1928), which do not require extended analysis; nor Virginia Woolf's *Orlando* (1928), a hermaphroditic romp through history, which is too fantastic for a study of this kind; nor Djuna Barnes' *Nightwood* (1936), which is vitiated by pretentious 'poetic' obscurity[3].

The naturalistic and documentary descriptions in the works of contemporary writers like Jean Genet and William Burroughs, John Rechy and Hubert Selby, are very different from the novels discussed in this book. They concern the homosexual's acts and not his mind, and appeal to sensation rather than to imagination. Genet's epics of masturbation and Burroughs' accounts of sexual cannibalism isolate the theme from the social context and deliberately abandon the very qualities of subtlety, ambiguity and restraint that distinguish the artistic greatness of the earlier works. When the laws of obscenity were changed and homosexuality became legal, apologies seemed inappropriate, the theme surfaced defiantly and sexual acts were grossly described. The emancipation of the homosexual has led, paradoxically, to the decline of his art.

II

Homosexuality is a rather vague and frequently misunderstood term that is generally defined as sexual desire for or relations between members of the same sex, but it may extend from repressed and unconscious longings to an active participation in sodomy. The literature of homosexuality begins with the Book of Genesis, which portrays the Sodomites as evil men who want to rape visitors and violate the tradition of hospitality. When the Lord sent two angels to Sodom to find ten righteous men who could save the wicked city from destruction, they were invited into Lot's house and feasted with him. Before they lay down to sleep the house was surrounded by the men of the city:

> And they called unto Lot, and said unto him, Where are the men which came in to thee this night? bring them out unto us, that we may know them. And Lot went out at the door unto them, and shut the door after him, And said, I pray you, brethren, do not so wickedly. Behold now, I have two daughters which have not known man; let me, I pray you, bring them out unto you, and do ye to them as is good in your eyes: only unto these men do nothing. (Genesis 19: 5-8)

But the single-minded Sodomites were not tempted by the bribe of virgins and continued to assault the house until the angels blinded them. The righteous men were never found, and the cities of the plain were totally destroyed by the fire and brimstone of the avenging Lord[4].

Though homosexuality has been considered both a disease and a crime, the legal definition was necessarily more precise than the medical; and the penalties, until very recently, were both inhumane and ineffective. On the ancient authority of Leviticus 20: 13 — 'If a man also lie with mankind, as he lieth with a woman, both of them have committed an abomination: they shall surely be put to death; their blood shall be upon them' — anal intercourse was punishable by death in England until 1828, and sentences were actually carried out as late as 1811. Smollett laments in *Roderick Random* (1748) that homosexuality 'gains ground apace and in all probability will become in a short time a more fashionable device than fornication'.[5]

And Taylor states that in the mid-nineteenth century — when male brothels (like Jupien's in Proust's novel) existed in London and were patronized by Swinburne — inversion 'was at least as common as in the eighteenth, despite the severer measures taken to repress' it.[6]

In 1885 the Criminal Law Amendment Act was passed to protect women and girls from procuration, and to suppress brothels; and the last-minute additions to this Act, which was not originally designed to punish male homosexuality, are summarized by Symonds:

> (1) Sodomy is a felony, defined as the carnal knowledge (per anum) of any man or of any woman by a male person; punishable with penal servitude for life as a maximum, for ten years as a minimum. (2) The attempt to commit sodomy is punishable with ten years' penal servitude as a maximum. (3) The commission, in public or in private, by a male person with another male person, of 'any act of gross indecency', is punishable with two years' imprisonment and hard labour.[7]

At the time of his trials in 1895 Oscar Wilde, who was charged under the third clause with committing acts of gross indecency in private, was at the height of his career. He had two plays running in the West End (both *An Ideal Husband* and *The Importance of Being Earnest* were closed when he was arrested), and was married with two children. Hyde believes that his peculiar habits were due to a recurrence of syphilis which he had caught from a prostitute while at Oxford and which forced him 'to discontinue physical relations with his wife'.[8] During the second trial, which ended with the jury's stalemate, the male prostitute Charles Parker testified with hypocritical indignation: 'I was asked by Wilde to imagine that I was a woman and that he was my lover. I had to keep up this illusion. I used to sit on his knees and he used to [play with my privates] as a man might amuse himself with a girl. Wilde insisted on this filthy make-believe being kept up.'[9] This fantasy was accompanied by mutual masturbation, intercrural intercourse and fellatio, the three most common forms of homosexuality, but 'there was no question of actual *pedicatio* being perpetrated'.[10] Wilde's famous and moving defence in this trial provided a powerful contrast to Parker's testimony, for it deliberately ignored the disparity between his sexual behaviour and platonic idealism, and emphasized the spiritual and intellectual aspects of male love which transcend carnal desire:

> 'The love that dare not speak its name' in this century is such a
> great affection of an elder for a younger man as there was between
> David and Jonathan, such as Plato made the very basis of his
> philosophy, and such as you find in the sonnets of Michelangelo
> and Shakespeare. It is that deep, spiritual affection that is as pure as
> it is perfect . . . It is beautiful, it is fine, it is the noblest form of
> affection. There is nothing unnatural about it. It is intellectual,
> and it repeatedly exists between an elder and a younger man,
> when the elder man has intellect, and the younger man has all the
> joy, hope and glamour of life before him.[11]

Despite the fact that Wilde's accusers were not only his sexual
accomplices but also self-confessed blackmailers who were obviously testifying against him to avoid prosecution, Justice Wills
embellished his sentence with an outraged and vitriolic speech that
reflected the fearful and irrational revulsion against inversion:

> [I have] the utmost sense of indignation at the horrible charges
> brought home to you . . . You, Wilde, have been the centre of a
> circle of extensive corruption of the most hideous kind among
> young men . . . I shall, under such circumstances, be expected to
> pass the severest sentence that the law allows. In my judgment it is
> totally inadequate for such a case as this.[12]

The violent attack on Wilde by the London *Evening News* on the day
of his conviction was similar to newspaper attacks later made on Sir
Roger Casement after his conviction, and helps to explain why
middle class opinion condemned not only homosexuals, but also
homosexual art:

> [Wilde] was one of the high priests of a school which attacks all
> the wholesome, manly, simple ideals of English life, and sets up
> false gods of decadent culture and intellectual debauchery. The
> man himself was a perfect type of his class, a gross sensualist
> veneered with the affectation of artistic feeling too delicate for the
> apprehension of common clay . . . We venture to hope that the
> conviction of Wilde for these abominable vices, which were the
> natural outcome of his diseased intellectual condition, will be a

salutary warning to the unhealthy boys who passed as sharers of his culture.[13]

Wilde was condemned by his aristocratic fictional heroes and his 'decadent culture' was equated with his sexual perversion.

During the first, Queensberry, trial the prosecutor Edward Carson (who reappeared twenty years later as Casement's political enemy) cross-examined Wilde on the dubious morality of Dorian Gray and his friend Basil Hallward. Carson read to the jury Hallward's confession of passion for Dorian, which appeared in the serialized version of 1890 but was omitted from Chapter 9 when the book was published the following year (the deleted sentences are in italics):

> *It's quite true that I have worshipped you with far more romance of feeling than a man usually gives to a friend. Somehow, I have never loved a woman* . . . From the moment I met you, your personality had the most extraordinary influence over me. *I quite admit that I adored you madly, extravagantly, absurdly.* I was jealous of every one to whom you spoke. I wanted to have you all to myself. I was only happy when I was with you.

Carson then challenged Wilde, who was very careful not to be explicit about what was nevertheless obvious, 'Does not this passage suggest a charge of unnatural vice?' And the accused coolly responded, 'It describes Dorian Gray as a man of very corrupt influence, though there's no statement as to the nature of that influence'.[14]

Frank Harris says (with considerable exaggeration) that after Wilde's arrest 'every train to Dover was crowded; every steamer to Calais was thronged with members of the aristocratic and leisured classes, who seemed to prefer Paris, or even Nice out of season, to a city like London where the police might act with such unexpected vigour'.[15] The Continent was undoubtedly more tolerant than England, for the Napoleonic Code of 1810 (and the Italian Penal Code of 1889) did not punish adult homosexuality.[16] As Joe Ackerley (who was something of a connoisseur) observed: 'Paris, Copenhagen, Stockholm, Vienna, Budapest, all provide their stage-nudes, brothels, bars, locales, Turkish Baths, cabarets and the rest of it . . . The Danes make only two stipulations: there is a strict age limit (I forget what it is) for boys and girls [18 years], and people must not misbehave in public.'[17] Although adult homosexuality was legal on the Continent, it was still taboo and a strong feeling of moral condemnation prevailed. Like Verlaine before him, Proust never openly admitted his inversion. Gide's courageous *apologia*, *Corydon*, written in 1911, was not published until 1923; and he was forced to delete revealing passages from *If It Die* (1926) when the second edition came out in 1934.

Wilde's conviction was followed by a number of other sensational homosexual scandals, both in England and on the Continent, whose victims often chose to kill themselves rather than face the inevitable social condemnation and legal conviction. The arms magnate, Friedrich Krupp, lived apart from his wife in a pleasure palace on Capri. When local complaints were investigated in 1902, a story appeared in the Italian newspapers, photographs proved that he had seduced boys and he was forced to leave the country. When the German newspapers took up the scandal, despite the government's attempt at suppression, Krupp's homosexual adventures led to repression in Germany in the same way as Wilde's trial had done in England.

In 1903 General Sir Hector Macdonald, who had risen from the rank of private after a brilliant military career in India and South Africa, was accused of homosexuality in Ceylon. After being brought to London, denounced and ordered back to Ceylon to face a court-martial, he shot himself in a Paris hotel room. In 1906 Phillip, Prince Eulenberg, the German diplomat, statesman and intimate friend of the Kaiser, was arraigned on charges of homosexuality, but let off when his health collapsed under the strain. In *Cities of the Plain* the Baron de Charlus,

> who was irresistibly drawn by his own tendencies to the Eulenberg affair, remembered what one of the most highly placed of the culprits had said to him: 'The Emperor must have relied upon our delicacy to have dared to allow such a trial. But he was not mistaken in trusting to our discretion. We would have gone to the scaffold with our lips sealed.'[18]

In 1913 Alfred Redl, a colonel in the Austrian military intelligence, was blackmailed for homosexuality and forced to reveal vital secrets to the Russians. But when Redl, the subject of John Osborne's play,

A Patriot For Me (1965), was discovered, the military code of honour allowed him to commit suicide. And Roger Casement's execution for high treason in 1916 was probably due to the public revelations about his inversion, which he carefully recorded in his notorious Black Diaries.[19]

Modern English literature was significantly affected by the conviction of Wilde in 1895, for it established the pattern of persecution that forced homosexuals to go underground for more than seventy years. The postwar period in England led to more liberal attitudes about the relations of men and women, but not about inversion. Though lesbianism had never been illegal, *The Well of Loneliness* was banned as obscene after a scandalous trial in 1928.[20] As late as 1942, during a homosexual trial of twenty men in Wales, 'one youth of nineteen committed suicide on the railway lines, and two others attempted unsuccessfully to do away with themselves by hanging and poison, to avoid the shame of exposure . . . The savage sentences, up to and including ten years' penal servitude, [were] allowed by the law and imposed by the judge.'[21]

The laws against inversion remained in force until the recommendations of the widely publicized Wolfenden Report (1957) — which advised that (as before 1885) 'homosexual behaviour between consenting adults in private should no longer be a criminal offence'[22] — were embodied in the Sexual Offences Act of 1967. Although the law was changed in England and Wales, homosexuality is still illegal in Scotland, Ireland, the armed forces and the merchant navy.

Adult homosexuality is no longer a crime, but it is still considered a disease by many doctors. Freud thought it was a sign of arrested development and categorized it as a pathological condition. And most contemporary psychoanalysts, though tolerant, tend to believe it is a functional disorder rather than a variant of 'normal' sexual behaviour. As Bieber writes: 'A homosexual adaptation is a result of "hidden but incapacitating fears of the opposite sex" . . . Any adaptation which is basically an accommodation to unrealistic fear is necessarily pathologic.'[23]

In the Victorian age the great writers like Dickens, Thackeray, Tennyson and Browning were also the popular ones, but at the end of the nineteenth century homosexual literature seemed to typify the divorce between the modern artist and the rest of society. This opposition is expressed in the series of polarities that frequently appear in homosexual novels. These books are necessarily élitist, for they deal with unusual and even repulsive characters, are elusive and difficult, and deliberately address themselves to the precious few. The homosexual writer in the modern period is analogous to the tubercular artist, like Schiller and Keats, in the eighteenth and nineteenth centuries, for inversion, like disease, puts its mark on a high percentage of artists and sets them apart from society. Homosexuality, like tuberculosis, seems to stimulate creative genius,[24] for the constant anxiety, fear and sense of doom intensifies isolation and introspection, heightens the intellectual defiance of the social outcast who is forced to question and challenge conventional ideas about morality and art, and encourages him to control the potentially dangerous element in his character through the order and form of art. As Nietzsche writes, 'one must still have chaos in oneself to be able to give birth to a dancing star'.[25]

III

The fear of social condemnation and judicial punishment forced homosexuals to assume a protective posture in life and to devise a strategy of art that would allow them to express their private feelings in a public genre. Like Oscar Wilde, they desperately and defensively cite the moral examples and aesthetic principles of ancient Israel and classical Greece to justify, rationalize or condone the validity of their personal obsessions.

Despite the notorious behaviour and dreadful punishment of the inhabitants of the cities of the plain, homosexual writers exploit the biblical contrast between the wicked Sodomites and the poetic love of David and Jonathan, and invoke the youths as the Hebrew archetypes (Achilles and Patroclus are the Homeric models) of passionate male friendship. Both Gide and D. H. Lawrence wrote plays on this biblical theme and must have appreciated the sexual symbolism of Jonathan's confession to Saul: 'I did but taste a little honey with the end of the rod that was in mine hand, and, lo, I must die' (I Samuel 14: 43). Wilde enthusiastically exclaims that Gide 'has written an astonishing play on Saul, whose madness he ascribes to his helpless love for David, and his wild jealousy of Jonathan'.[26] And in a review of *David* (1926), Edward Sackville-West compares

Gide's hero to Proust's and contrasts his treatment of the story with Lawrence's:

> [Gide] makes of Saul a sort of feeble Baron de Charlus, assailed by the demons of neurosis (brought on to the stage), and the interest of the play is frankly erotic. Mr Lawrence's Jonathan is rather a strong character, a 'lithe stripling', and in his relations with David he takes the ascendant. M. Gide, on the other hand, sees him as a beautiful fainting, effeminate creature, in a state of hysterical rapture over David's physical strength.[27]

Like the love of David and Jonathan, homosexuality in classical Greece was openly practised, and it was universally accepted as one of the fundamental pleasures of life. Both the *Symposium* and *Phaedrus* glorify love between a man and a boy or a younger man. Phaedrus says in the *Symposium*: 'I know not any greater blessing to a young man who is beginning life than a virtuous lover, or to the lover than a beloved youth'; and in the *Phaedrus* Socrates states (in Jowett's rather hazy Victorian translation): 'Thus fair and blissful to the beloved is the desire of the inspired lover, and the initiation of which I speak into the mysteries of true love, if he be captured by the lover and their purpose is effected'.[28]

Plato strongly influenced the morality of both the teachers and the pupils in the public schools. The sanctification of the Classics, which had a far stronger influence than they have today, provided a poetic model of behaviour, made love between youths acceptable and led to an elimination — or at least a reduction — of guilt. Forster, for example, writes of his hero, Maurice:

> Never could he forget his emotion at first reading the *Phaedrus*. He saw there his malady described exquisitely, calmly, as a passion which we can direct, like any other, towards good or bad. Here was no invitation to license. He could not believe his good fortune at first — thought there must be some misunderstanding and that he and Plato were thinking of different things. Then he saw that the temperate pagan really did comprehend him, and, slipping past the Bible rather than opposing it, was offering a new guide for life.[29]

Virtually all public school boys had homosexual experience. After Wilde's conviction the journalist W. T. Stead wrote: 'If all persons guilty of Oscar Wilde's offences were to be clapped in gaol, there would be a very surprising exodus from Eton and Harrow, Rugby and Winchester, to Pentonville and Holloway'.[30] Many boys prolonged their adolescent homosexuality indefinitely when they entered the Army (like T. E. Lawrence) or the colonial service (like Roger Casement) and continued to live in an exclusively masculine milieu.

Yet homosexual writers have also criticized the attempt to extinguish guilt and shame by idealizing the morality of a remote civilization. Auden points out an important qualification that is often ignored by platonic apologists: 'Ancient Greece and Rome were both pederastic cultures in which the adult passive homosexual was regarded as comic and contemptible'.[31] And both Byron and Proust ridicule platonic love. In *Don Juan* the bisexual poet portrays the philosopher as a pander to sexual immorality:

> Oh Plato! Plato! you have paved the way,
>   With your confounded fantasies, to more
> Immoral conduct by the fancied sway
>   Your system feigns o'er the controlless core
> Of human hearts, than all the long array
>   Of poets and romancers: — You're a bore,
> A charlatan, a coxcomb — and have been
>   At best, no better than a go-between. (I. cxvi)

And in *Cities of the Plain* Proust satirizes the concept of historical justification by carrying it to a logical but absurd conclusion and casually alluding to the hermaphroditic theory of sexual genesis propounded in the *Symposium*:

> The race of inverts who eagerly connect themselves with Oriental antiquity [the Bible] or the Golden Age in Greece, might be traced back further still to those experimental epochs in which there existed neither dioecious plants nor monosexual animals, to that initial hermaphroditism of which certain rudiments of male organs in the anatomy of the woman and of female organs in that of the man seem still to preserve the trace.[32]

Reade writes that '1894 could be described as a golden year for homosexuals in England, for the very reason that it was the last year for a long time in which they could take shelter in public ignorance or tolerance to propagate a non-hostile climate of taste and opinion'.[33] The first sign of a more sympathetic attitude toward inversion appeared in the 1860s in the works of Karl Heinrich Ulrichs, a German sexologist who coined the term *Urning* for homosexual. Privately printed books like John Addington Symonds' *A Problem in Modern Ethics* (1891), Edward Carpenter's *Homogenic Love* (1894) and Marc-André Raffalovich's *Uranisme et Unisexualité* (1896) were the first to idealize homosexuality, while Havelock Ellis' *Sexual Inversion* (1897) brought the subject into the open and discussed it with clinical objectivity.

Edward Carpenter (1844-1929) was an important influence on both Forster and D. H. Lawrence.[34] In his courageous but rather soppy book he appeals not only to biblical and platonic authority, but also to the contemporary prophet, Walt Whitman, who romanticized homosexuality as 'comradeship' and 'adhesiveness', and helped to evolve a language of male love that would distinguish it from the conventions of heterosexual romance. Carpenter, in a surprising aesthetic judgment that suggests special pleading, calls the undisciplined and self-indulgent Whitman 'the most Greek in spirit and in performance of modern writers, [who] insists continually on this social function of "intense and loving comradeship, the personal and passionate attachment of man to man"'.[35]

Wilde's defiant profligacy, and what the *Evening News* called his 'intellectual debauchery' and 'affection of artistic feeling', seemed to characterize the snobbish, aesthetic, precious, sensitive, singular, subversive and overtly homosexual aspect of the high art, rarefied culture and platonic idealism of the 1890s. Wilde quite deliberately opposed the jolly humour of J. K. Jerome and W. W. Jacobs, the rugged romances of Rider Haggard and Robert Louis Stevenson, the Fabian heartiness of Shaw and Wells, and the 'wholesome, manly ideals' of Kipling, Henley and the Victorian empire-builders. Wilde, who met 'Bosie' Douglas and compacted his tragic destiny in 1891, two months after he published *The Picture of Dorian Gray*, was the first novelist to defy literary convention and to write about homosexuality in a manner that was obvious to the sophisticated reader. He burst the restrictive barriers, and the others followed in his wake.

IV

The Picture of Dorian Gray is the *locus classicus* of the modern homosexual novel, and Wilde's sensitivity and luxury, his refined taste and lapidary prose, his decadence and neurasthenia, and his desire to escape from the vulgarity of the contemporary world, are all reflected in the novels of Gide, Mann and Proust. Wilde had a personal as well as a literary influence on Gide, who was dazzled by his brilliant conversation but found his style derivative and affected:

> *Dorian Gray* in its conception was a wonderful story, far superior to [Balzac's] *La Peau de Chagrin*, and far more significant! Alas! when written, what a masterpiece spoiled. In his most delightful tales literary influence makes itself too much felt . . . The result is that one's emotion is held at bay, and the dazzling of the surface so blinds one's eyes and mind, that the deep central emotion is lost.[36]

Both *Dorian Gray* and *The Immoralist*, despite their attempts to idealize inversion (the 'central emotion') and create a new system of morality, suggest it is impossible to achieve homosexual pleasure without the inevitable accompaniment of fear, guilt and self-hatred. Despite his bitter truths about inversion, the French writer was enormously important to Forster, who 'wept to hear of the death of André Gide, not for personal reasons, he knew him only slightly, but because he felt that one of the great props of his own civilization had been withdrawn'.[37]

Both *The Immoralist* and *Death in Venice* are influenced by Nietzsche and emphasize the destructive side of homosexuality. Mann sees Gide as a kind of successful Aschenbach 'who won out over guilt and neurosis through the discipline of his art, for whom this art had become the saving instrument of self-control, and for whom language and style had turned into the blessed remedies for the anarchy within'.[38] Mann asserts the superiority of Gide's *The Counterfeiters* and rather harshly asks: 'Isn't *The Immoralist* of 1902 a first novel of rather faded originality, whose capacity to shock has largely been lost through the decades, and whose title, inspired by Nietzsche, smothers the content by sheer philosophical dead weight?'[39]

But unlike Wilde and Gide, Mann's classical idealization of

inversion is completely ironic. Yet D. H. Lawrence seems unaware of Mann's irony and in his review of *Death in Venice* makes the fundamental error of equating Mann with Aschenbach: 'It is absolutely, almost intentionally unwholesome. The man is sick body and soul. He portrays himself as he is, with wonderful skill and art, portrays . . . one man, one atmosphere, one sick vision'.[40] In *Death in Venice* and *Young Törless* the homosexual theme is overt rather than covert, as in Wilde and Gide. In Mann's novella inversion represents the possibility of self-destruction inherent in creative genius, and in Musil's book (as in *Billy Budd* and 'The Prussian Officer') it symbolizes the cruelty of power.

Musil's portrayal of the sado–masochistic aspects of perversion foreshadows the painful self-scrutiny of Proust and T. E. Lawrence. Proust's Introduction to *Cities of the Plain*, which considers the modern descendents of the inhabitants of Sodom, is a most thorough and perceptive analysis of the psychology of homosexuals and their role in society. The puritanical Gide, who records in his *Journals*: 'My most recent adventures have filled me with an inexpressible disgust',[41] was surprised by Proust's personal — as opposed to public — openness about his tendencies. Gide writes that 'Far from denying or hiding his homosexuality, [Proust] exhibits it, and I could almost say boasts of it. He claims never to have loved women save spiritually, and never to have known love except with men.'[42] But Proust's literary objectivity and detachment are sometimes compromised by his self-hatred, which manifests itself in a moral and censorious tone that is diametrically opposed to the idealized portraits of Wilde and Gide as well as of Forster and D. H. Lawrence. Proust satirizes the exterior stigmata of vice and writes, for example, in his anatomy of the wealthy and aristocratic society in Jupien's brothel: 'The aspect of [inverts] inspired a repugnance due, doubtless, to their indulging in degrading vices.'[43]

Gide's conversation with Proust at the end of his life led him to an acute insight about the latter's fascination with the perversions of Charlus, for he notes that Proust 'shows himself to be very much concerned when I tell him that he seems to have wanted to stigmatize homosexuality; he protests; and eventually I understand that what we consider vile, an object of laughter or disgust, does not seem so repulsive to him'.[44] Forster stresses Proust's complete pessimism and says that 'Despair underlies all his view of personal relationships.

How he emphasizes the element of gratuitous cruelty that exists in us
. . . What repulsive defects he discovers in us! The worst of them is
our inability to love or be loved.'[45]

Though Conrad was not himself a homosexual, he was forced to
treat this theme in a covert manner. Like Mann and Musil, Conrad
does not attempt to idealize or justify inversion in *Victory;* and he
uses Jones' sexual corruption as a metaphor for social evil, and
Heyst's repressed homosexuality and fear of human emotions to
symbolize the conflict between isolation and integration.

Unlike Wilde, Gide and Proust, who deliberately defy society,
Forster is a liberal humanist who shares its basic values, hides his
inversion and finds it difficult to express his most intense and
personal feelings. As he records in his diary of 1964: 'I should have
been a more famous writer if I had written or rather published more,
but sex has prevented the latter'.[46] After a well-intentioned but rather
insensitive attempt to re-fashion Forster in his own image, Lawrence
writes to Bertrand Russell in 1915:

> We have had E. M. Forster here for three days. There is more in
> him than ever comes out. But he is not dead yet. I hope to see him
> pregnant with his own soul. We were on the edge of a fierce
> quarrel all the time . . . I liked him, but his life is so ridiculously
> inane, the man is dying of inanition. He was very angry with me
> for telling him about himself . . . He tries to dodge himself — the
> sight is pitiful.[47]

In *Where Angels Fear to Tread, The Longest Journey* and especially *A
Room With A View*, the disguised homosexual theme subtly
undermines the heterosexual romance. But in the posthumously
published *Maurice*, which was written in 1913-14, and in *The Life to
Come*, Forster abandons the ironic detachment from his personal
feelings, and makes a therapeutic and didactic attempt to glorify
homosexual love.

The close friendship of Forster and T. E. Lawrence was based on
their homosexual sympathy.[48] When Forster first read the manu-
script of *Seven Pillars of Wisdom* he was impressed by its frankness and
copied out two striking descriptions of homosexual encounters. 'If
you knew all about me', Lawrence wrote to him from India in 1927,
'(perhaps you do: your subtlety is very great: shall I put it "if I knew
that you knew . . ."?) you'd think very little of me. And I wouldn't

like to feel I was on the way to being able to know about you.'[49] Both men hid behind their natural reserve and felt much safer that way. Lawrence's phrase, 'if you knew *all* about me', probably refers to the masochistic and cruel side of his character that Forster did not really know. But he had observed that Lawrence did not like to be touched and 'had some queer friends', whom Forster instinctively distrusted. Though Forster was more conventional, fearful and repressed, Lawrence's homosexuality was more destructive, and could be satisfied only by the whippings that punished the guilt for his submission at Deraa, tested the body and defiantly reaffirmed the power of the will. The central chapters of *Seven Pillars of Wisdom*, examine the relation of sexual pathology to the Nietzschean will that enabled him to achieve his military triumphs and led, ironically, to his personal defeat.

In a review of D. H. Lawrence's novels, T. E. Lawrence quotes his suggestive quatrain from 'Ballad of a Wilful Woman':

> While a naked man comes swiftly
> Like a spurt of white foam, rent
> From the crest of a falling breaker,
> Over the poppies sent,

emphasizes his sensuality, and calls him a 'poet, and thinker, a man exquisitely a-tingle to every throb of blood, flexure of sinew, plane-modulation of the envelope of flesh'.[50] Forster's analysis of the major themes of D. H. Lawrence's *Pornography and Obscenity* reveals the contrast between his own repressive and D. H. Lawrence's expressive attitude toward sex, and suggests a central weakness in Forster's novels:

> To him the one evil is 'self-enclosure,' and under this definition he includes not merely the physical act of masturbation, but any emotional counterpart of it, any turning-inward upon itself of the spirit, any furtiveness and secrecy, any tendency to live in little private circles of excitement, rather than in the passionate outer life of personal interchange.[51]

After D. H. Lawrence's death in 1930, Forster challenged contemporary opinion and called him 'the greatest imaginative novelist of our generation'.[52] And in his generous obituary notice, Forster described his intense admiration for Lawrence, though he was sceptical about his utopian schemes and rather frightened by the ferocious prophet who had tried to make him 'pregnant with his own soul':

> In the spring of 1915 I met him three or four times. I did not know him well, or meet him again subsequently, but he leaves a vivid impression — so quick with his fingers and alive in his spirit, so radiant and sensitive, so sure that if we all set out at once for one of the South Sea Islands we should found a perfect community there which would regenerate the world. Shelley must have been a little like that, but Lawrence was a rougher, tougher proposition than Shelley; there is a vein of cruelty in him.[53]

Lawrence's desire to examine every aspect of his own character and every possibility of human fulfilment inevitably led him to an exploration of homosexuality, though his trust and belief in the instinct, the body and the blood is a strong contrast to T. E. Lawrence's masochism and renunciation. *The White Peacock, Women in Love, Aaron's Rod* and *The Plumed Serpent,* which reveal his streak of cruelty, describe several mutually destructive conflicts between men and women, and an alternative search for satisfactory masculine relationships

In the modern period homosexuals became an important literary subject, for writers were attracted to the stigmata of the feared, hated and persecuted outsider who defied the moral law, subverted the concept of the family, symbolized the destructive element in passion and threatened the virility of the ordinary man. The homosexual experience portrayed in modern literature is extremely negative, for even Forster's happy endings are completely unconvincing. Gide's Michel lapses into boredom and apathy as he tastes the 'fruit filled with bitter ashes'; Musil's Törless is forced to leave school and returns home bitterly disillusioned and estranged from his family; Proust's Charlus, betrayed and abandoned, decays into disgusting decrepitude; and the quest of D. H. Lawrence's heroes for male friendship leads to failure and to sodomy with women. Wilde's Dorian Gray commits suicide; Mann's Aschenbach submits to death by cholera; Conrad's Heyst burns himself to death; and T. E. Lawrence's torture and rape at Deraa end in a physical and mental breakdown.

The grave sexual and social problems that affect the lives of homosexuals and often lead to unhappiness and tragedy have been analysed by Auden and Baldwin. The poet writes in his review of Ackerley's *My Father and Myself*: 'Few, if any, homosexuals can boast that their sex life has been happy . . . The eternal and, probably, insoluble problem for the homosexual is finding a substitute for the natural differences, anatomical and psychic, between a man and a woman.'[54] And the novelist's essay on Gide echoes Forster's comments on the loveless despair of Proust: 'The really terrible thing about the phenomenon of present-day homosexuality . . . is that today's unlucky deviate can only save himself by the most tremendous exertion of all his forces from falling into an underworld in which he never meets either man or woman, where it is impossible to have either a lover or a friend, where the possibility of a genuine human involvement has altogether ceased'.[55]

II

WILDE

The Picture of Dorian Gray

For any man of culture to accept the standard of his age is a form of the grossest immorality.

The Picture of Dorian Gray

Most critics of *The Picture of Dorian Gray* (1891) treat the book as a classical illustration of literary aestheticism and decadence or, like Roditi, concentrate on its heterogeneous sources, from the Gothic novel through Balzac and Poe to Pater and Huysmans.[1] Despite the abundant evidence, both external and internal, no critic has discussed the work as a homosexual novel. But this interpretation defines more precisely the nature of its decadence and its relation to Baudelaire and *Against Nature*; reveals a coherence and consistency in the uneven, loosely structured, melodramatic and sometimes absurd work; and suggests that the real meaning of the novel, like so many others on this subject, is more complex and interesting than it appears to be. It is really about the jealousy and pain, the fear and guilt of being a homosexual.

The most recent biographer of Wilde writes that the models for two of the principal characters in the novel were notorious homosexuals. Basil Hallward was 'Charles Shannon, the artist who for many years lived in marital bliss with Charles Ricketts, and Lord Henry Wotton . . . was Lord Ronald Gower', whom Croft-Cooke calls 'a thorough-paced queer who liked rough trade and found time, in spite of a public career, to enjoy it prodigally'.[2] Wilde himself emphasizes that the characters are also projections of his own personality and says that *Dorian Gray* 'contains much of me. Basil Hallward is what I think I am: Lord Henry what the world thinks of me: Dorian what I would like to be — in other ages, perhaps'.[3] Wilde thinks he is an artist and an idealist who loves beauty and handsome young men, and wants to be inspired by them as Socrates was

inspired by Alcibiades. The world, encouraged by his wicked
persona, believes he is a posturing, dissolute cynic. Wilde would like
to be a beautiful youth, and he would also like to enjoy homosexual
love without the severe and repressive legal penalties of the late
Victorian age. For as Dorian

> looked back upon man moving through History, he was haunted
> by a feeling of loss. So much had been surrendered! and to such
> little purpose! There had been mad wilful rejections, monstrous
> forms of self-torture and self-denial, whose origin was fear, and
> whose result was a degradation infinitely more terrible than that
> fancied degradation from which, in their ignorance, they had
> sought to escape.[4]

Wilde's condemnation of the repression of homosexuals — who are
not specifically mentioned though they are clearly the subject of this
passage — anticipates Freud's ideas about the irremediable antagon-
ism between the demands of instinct and the restrictions of
civilization in *Civilization and Its Discontents* (1930). Wotton also
believes that repression is evil and argues that 'the only way to get rid
of a temptation is to yield to it. Resist it, and your soul grows sick
with longing for the things it has forbidden to itself, with desire for
what its monstrous laws have made monstrous and unlawful' (25-6).
In the novel Hallward and Wotton, the artistic and cynical aspects of
Wilde, personify Dorian's conscience and instinct, the irresolvable
conflict between his superego and his id.

But this triple projection of Wilde's personality leads to a split
between the characters and the ideas they are meant to represent. The
kindly and optimistic Hallward seems to come closest to the ideal of
the novel — 'to teach man to concentrate himself upon the moments
of a life that is itself but a moment . . . [and] find in the spiritualizing
of the senses its highest realization'. But Hallward is killed by
Dorian, whose descent into the 'vulgar profligacy' that dulls the
senses and into the suicide that extinguishes them is the antithesis of
the ideal that Wilde is trying to express through Hallward. The ideas
of Wotton, who urges Dorian to realize his true nature and yield to
temptation even though his passions might shame him, are
discredited by Dorian's dissolute behaviour. Wotton epigram-
matically expresses some fine and some bitter sentiments, but we
cannot take him seriously because he is an essentially passive and

negative character who vicariously experiences evil through Dorian and has no real life of his own. We are constantly told about the evil of Dorian, who also enjoys corrupting young men, but we never learn exactly what he has done because the theme cannot be overtly expressed and the characters hide as much as they reveal.

The original inspiration for the novel also evolved from Wilde's personal experience:

> When the sitting was over and Mr Wilde had looked at his portrait, it occurred to him that a thing of beauty, when it takes the form of a middle-aged gentleman, is unhappily not a joy forever. 'What a tragic thing it is', he exclaimed. 'This portrait will never grow old, and I shall.' Then the passion of his soul sought refuge in prose composition, and the result was 'Dorian Gray'.[5]

This autobiographical incident is transposed directly into the novel when Dorian, staring at his finished portrait, remarks: 'How sad it is! I shall grow old, and horrible, and dreadful. But this picture will remain always young . . . If it were only the other way! If it were I who was to be always young, and the picture that was to grow old! . . . I would give my soul for that!' (33). This fanciful yet fatal wish for eternal youth and beauty (since old age is horrible and dreadful), rather than for moral or intellectual or artistic qualities, is consummated by a devil's pact in which the face on the canvas bears the burdens of his passions and his sins in return for a final, Gothic retribution. This pact turns Dorian into an image without a soul and allows him to be loved by men (and women) without having to love them in return.

The opening paragraphs of the novel, with their evocation of opium-tainted cigarettes and Baudelairean *fleurs du mal* (an anodyne for pain that becomes a recurrent theme in the book, for Dorian sniffs a flower just before he murders Hallward), establishes an atmosphere of preciosity and corruption. And this ambience is reinforced by Hallward's description of his first meeting and subsequent relationship with Dorian:

> When our eyes first met I felt I was growing pale. A curious sensation of terror came over me. I knew that I had come face to face with someone whose mere personality was so fascinating

that, if I allowed it to do so, it would absorb my whole nature, my whole *soul*, my very art itself . . . I have always been my own master; had at least always been so, till I met Dorian Gray. Then . . . something seemed to tell me that I was on the verge of a terrible crisis in my life. I had a strange feeling that Fate had in store for me exquisite joys and exquisite sorrows. (12)

Though Dorian is young, innocent and beautiful — 'a type that was to combine something of the real culture of the scholar with all the grace and distinction and perfect manner of a citizen of the world' — Hallward's first, intensely physical reaction, is of fear. And though Dorian's character has not yet come under Wotton's evil influence, Hallward immediately feels threatened, weak and subservient as he enters the sexual crisis that provides far more sorrows than joys.

Hallward enjoys confessing his literal idolatry and admits, 'I couldn't be happy if I didn't see him every day. He is absolutely necessary to me'. He compares his love for Dorian to the love of Michelangelo, of Winckelmann (whom Pater discussed in *The Renaissance*), and of Shakespeare (whose passion for the young man of the Sonnets is described by Wilde in his story, 'The Portrait of Mr W. H.'). Hallward needs Dorian not only as an artistic inspiration, but also as the dominant partner in their sado-masochistic relationship; and he explains that 'Dorian's whims are laws to everybody, except himself . . . He is horribly thoughtless, and seems to take a real delight in giving me pain'.

When Wotton (the corrupt homosexual) maliciously steals Dorian from Hallward (the idealistic homosexual), the latter is forced to make humiliating though ineffectual pleas for Dorian's company. As he had foreseen, his art declines as his passionate friendship ends, and as Dorian becomes weary of 'the painter's absurd fits of jealousy, his wild devotion, his extravagant panegyrics, his curious reticences' (131).

Lord Henry Wotton[6] is supposed to represent cynical hedonism, but as Hallward justly remarks (paraphrasing Rochester's famous epigram on Charles II who 'never says a foolish thing, nor ever does a wise one'). 'You never say a moral thing, and you never do a wrong thing. Your cynicism is simply a pose.' If Hallward is the masochistic creator of Dorian's aesthetic glorification, Wotton (who manipulates the vanity stimulated by the portrait) is the sadistic catalyst of his moral degeneration.

Wotton is an extreme misogynist who intensifies the homosexual theme by insisting on the need to escape from the horrible *ennui* of fashionable society ('My dear fellow, she tried to found a *salon*, and only succeeded in opening a restaurant'), from the overwhelming dreariness of heterosexual relations, and from the tedium of marriage, a 'bad habit' whose one charm is that it 'makes a life of deception absolutely necessary for both parties'.

One of the subtlest scenes in the novel occurs when Wotton's wife first meets Dorian. Though she is a gauche and even ludicrous character, and an easy target for satire ('Her name was Victoria, and she had a perfect mania for going to church'), her awkward intrusion into her own library reveals her estrangement from Wotton and his intimacy with Dorian, whose photographs fill the house. Though Wilde writes, 'She was usually in love with somebody, and her passion was never returned', she causes a scandal by running away with her musical lover and divorcing Wotton. He deceives his wife with Dorian and appears indifferent to her infidelity; but she merely laughs at his affair, for his extreme passivity is the emotional equivalent of impotence.

Gray is inevitably compared to 'the perfection of the spirit that is Greek', to Greek marbles, a young Adonis and a Greek martyr (Hallward's masochistic projection) in order to create an aesthetic tradition for the homosexual ideal. Though he is more elaborately Corinthian than austerely Dorian, he takes his name from a race whom John Addington Symonds calls 'those martial founders of the institution of Greek love'.[7]

The correspondence between Dorian's external beauty and internal corruption is a variation of a more important Greek idea. According to the Neoplatonic doctrine expressed, for example, in Sidney's *Astrophel and Stella* (1580), the face is the outward form of the soul. Because of the harmony between the body and the soul, a beautiful face reveals an inward spirituality and inspires 'those whom Dante describes as having sought to "make themselves perfect by the worship of beauty"' (144). This same connection exists in *Dorian Gray*, where one character states that 'wicked people were always very old and very ugly', and where the grotesque reflection of Dorian's spiritual state is transferred to the painting.

Dorian's dualism is reflected in the attitudes of Hallward and Wotton. The former sees him as 'the visible incarnation of that unseen ideal whose memory haunts us artists like an exquisite dream', while the latter calls him the 'son of Love and Death'.

When Dorian attempts to love the young actress, Sibyl Vane, he ignores the warning in Juliet's speech: 'I have no joy of this contract tonight: / It is too rash, too unadvised, too sudden', and follows the pattern of Wotton's prediction: 'When one is in love, one always begins by deceiving oneself and one always ends by deceiving others'. Dorian deceives himself by believing that he is able to love a woman and that 'his unreal and selfish love would yield to some higher influence, would be *transformed* into some nobler passion'. He is attracted to Sibyl partly because she is an illusion who is idealized and distanced from him by the stage, and mainly because she is androgynous. For when she plays Rosalind in *As You Like It* she appeals to his homosexual tastes: 'she came out in her boy's clothes and was perfectly wonderful. She had never seemed to me more exquisite.'

Both Dorian and Sibyl have similarly sordid backgrounds which are meant to provide a melodramatic contrast to their youthful purity and to explain their bizarre behaviour. Both were children of a passionate but ill-considered love affair. When Dorian's father ran off with his mother, a beautiful heiress, he was forced into a duel and deliberately killed; and after the early death of Dorian's mother, the posthumous child was brought up by the same wicked grandfather who had arranged the duel and then replaced the man he had murdered. Sibyl was an illegitimate child whose father also died early in her life. His surrogate, at the time she meets Dorian, is a stereotyped 'hideous Jew' with greasy ringlets who has financial control over her and acts as her guardian and pander. The brief narration of their disturbed childhood attempts to account for their extreme sensitivity and vulnerability, their emotional instability, and their manic-depressive behaviour, for Dorian moves from adoration to hate and Sibyl from ecstasy to suicide. But none of these biographical details can make Dorian and Sibyl's relationship real, for the whole episode is merely symbolic.

Wilde suggests that Dorian rejects Sibyl when he discovers his preference for illusion to reality, and this polarity is similar to the art-life conflict expressed in Dorian's portrait. Hallward's early paintings of Dorian were 'unconscious, ideal and remote'; and when he first paints Dorian realistically, he reveals his love and Dorian's true nature, and destroys their friendship. Similarly, Dorian loves Sibyl as an actress, as an impersonator of romantic heroines in an unreal and artificial atmosphere. When her love for him freed her soul from her emotional prison and taught her to recognize reality, she saw the hollowness and sham of her empty performances. But when she began to 'live', she lost her ability to act and forced Dorian to accept her as a real woman, not as 'a dream or a phantom'. This change killed his 'love' because, in Huysmans' words, 'anyone who dreams of the ideal, prefers illusion to reality, and calls for veils to clothe the naked truth'.[8]

Dorian is never really in love with Sibyl because he is too narcissistic to love anyone but himself. He tries to love her because he believes it will be good for him to love a woman, but recoils when confronted with a real woman who loves him. Wilde associates reality with heterosexuality and illusion with homosexuality, and expresses Dorian's confirmation of his homosexuality through these associations. The ferocity of Dorian's reaction to Sibyl's love reveals the conflict between what he really feels and what society thinks he ought to feel.

Wilde derived these sexual and aesthetic associations from *Against Nature*, for Huysmans connects reality with bourgeois respectability and conventional morality, and equates art with imagination, refinement, sensuality and immoral love. In Huysmans and Wilde's scale of values homosexuality, which is anti-social and taboo, is related to art; and homosexuals surround themselves with rich and elaborate illusions to 'spiritualize the senses'.

Wotton completes his domination of Dorian by sending him a copy of *Against Nature* bound in yellow paper, for the 'whole book seemed to [Dorian] to contain the story of his own life, written before he had lived it'. Dorian responds passionately to Huysmans because he sanctifies the sensitive and *raffiné* mode of existence and provides an aesthetic justification of homosexuality. In view of Wilde's statement that *Dorian Gray* 'is a fantastic variation of Huysmans' over-realistic study of the artistic temperament in our unartistic age',[9] it is significant that Des Esseintes and Dorian are not real artists but dilettantes who express their artistic temperaments through Dandyism, hedonism (that is, childish self-indulgence) and

homosexuality. The whole of Chapter 11 is a weak imitation of
Huysmans, with successive paragraphs appropriately devoted to the
more *recherché* aspects of perfumes, music, jewels, embroideries and
ecclesiastical vestments, all used by Dorian as an aesthetic means of
escape from the guilt of his sexual perversity. Though Dorian, in
another weak attempt to rationalize his outrageous conduct,
complains that he was 'poisoned' by the book, it is clear that
Huysmans' novel did not change Dorian's life but merely accen-
tuated tendencies that already existed in him.

Auden observes in his review of Wilde's *Letters* that 'the artist and
the homosexual are both characterized by a greater-than-normal
amount of narcissism',[10] and this trait is particularly prominent in the
homosexual artist. Hallward rhapsodically tells Dorian: 'You had
leant over the still pool of some Greek woodland, and seen in the
water's silent silver the marvel of your own face'. And 'once, in
boyish mockery of Narcissus', Dorian had kissed his portrait. But
instead of falling in love, like Narcissus, with his own image, an
aesthetic extension of himself, he comes to hate it and destroys
himself as he attempts to destroy his portrait. In the modern age, the
relation of the artist to society has been analogous to the relation of
the homosexual to society, so that Dorian's image reflects his
self-hatred as well as his self-love.

The numerous parallels between Hallward and Sibyl also emphasize Dorian's homosexuality. He tells Wotton about his adoration of
Sibyl in the same way that Hallward told Wotton about his
idealization of Dorian. And Sibyl assumes Hallward's self-abasing
sexual posture, and expresses her love by flinging herself on her
knees, trembling all over 'like a white narcissus' and sobbing at
Dorian's feet. Hallward, who understands Dorian's true nature,
finds his engagement to Sibyl 'Impossible'. But on reflection,
though 'he could not bear this marriage, yet it seemed to him to be
better than many other things that might have happened'. These
other things could only refer to Dorian's liaison with another man.
By contrast, Dorian's mad adoration of Sibyl did not cause Wotton
the slightest pang of annoyance or jealousy because he knew that
Dorian could never love a woman.

Dorian's rejection of Sibyl is as sudden and unexpected as his
murder of Basil, and both crimes are inspired by the same motive.
For Basil and Sibyl (both have Greek names, though he is not regal

nor she prophetic) make a great emotional claim on Dorian who, because of the guilt about his homosexuality (the reason for his emphasis on purity), feels compelled to displace his self-hatred and to punish those who love him and attempt to redeem him. For Basil created the visible emblem of his conscience, and Sibyl's love might 'purify him, and shield him from those sins that seemed to be already stirring in spirit and in flesh — those curious *unpictured* sins whose very mystery lent them their subtlety and their charm' (137).

The irreconcilable conflict between art and life, between the homosexual and heterosexual modes of love, leads to the murder of Hallward just as it had led to the suicide of Sibyl and the corresponding signs of degeneration in Dorian's portrait. In the first chapter the artist says that he cannot exhibit the painting because 'I have put too much of myself into it', and he later adds that it would reveal the shameful secret of his idolatrous love for Dorian. The portrait also holds the secret of Dorian's life, for it teaches him to love his own beauty and to loathe his own soul, an impossible combination of homosexual narcissism and socially-conditioned self-hatred.

When Basil changes his mind and asks Dorian if he can exhibit the portrait, Dorian offers to exchange secrets about it. Though he discovers Hallward's secret, he never reveals his own until his friend visits him again on the night of the murder. Then, in response to the long sermon about his behaviour from Hallward, who has become an insufferable prig and a bore (and is killed, one suspects, partly for this reason), Dorian says, 'I shall show you my soul . . . You are the one man in the world entitled to know everything about me' — though Hallward already knows virtually everything there is to know. After revealing the visual evidence to Hallward and hearing his horrified response, Dorian is madly inspired by the overt image of evil and, pursuing a false logic, kills 'the friend who had painted the fatal portrait to which all his misery had been due'. It is significant that Dorian impulsively kills Hallward by driving a knife into the great *vein* behind the ear (the play in the novel on vein, vain and Vane is a weak attempt to achieve unity), and that he blackmails one of his homosexual acquaintances (who later commits suicide) and forces him to destroy the corpse with acid, for Sybil had also used prussic acid to destroy herself.[11]

Just as Basil haunts Dorian after his death through his portrait, so

Sibyl posthumously pursues him through her brother James, who has sworn to kill her deceiver. James is motivated by jealousy as well as by revenge, for in the absence of their father, he developed an unusually close and protective relationship with his sister. When he left for Australia they parted like lovers: 'her arms were flung round his neck, and her fingers strayed through his hair, and he softened, and kissed her with real affection'. After James, like Dorian's father, is conveniently shot (during a hunting party), the way is clear for Dorian to kill himself, as he had killed Hallward, by stabbing.

The crimes of desertion and murder are the external manifestations of the inward corruption that is frequently hinted at but never defined, and Dorian's subsequent absorption in evil is essentially homosexual. He shares a house with Wotton in Algiers (where Wilde enjoyed the pleasures of pederasty without fear of the law), adopts (like Sibyl) the 'curious disguises' of a transvestite, frequents the low dens that cater to the perverse predilections of foreign sailors, and acquires an impressive list of male victims:

> There was that wretched boy in the Guards who committed suicide. You were his great friend. There was Sir Henry Ashton, who had to leave England, with a tarnished name. You and he were inseparable. What about Adrian Singleton, and his dreadful end? What about Lord Kent's only son, and his career? I met his father yesterday in St. James's Street. He seemed broken with shame and sorrow. What about the young Duke of Perth? What sort of life has he got now? What gentleman would associate with him? (167-8).[12]

All these male friendships are described in terms of strong moral opprobrium — they are shameful, vile and degraded — and though Kent's son married a whore and Singleton forged a bill, all these men obviously practised what Lord Alfred Douglas called 'the love that dare not speak its name'.[13] Dorian has again punished a succession of well-born and promising young men for his own sin, which caused women who had wildly adored him 'to grow pallid with shame or horror if [he] entered the room'. These women felt shame for allowing themselves to be deceived by him, and horror of his vice. If Dorian were merely a libertine he would not be, as Hallward says, 'a man whom no pure-minded girl should be allowed to know, and whom no chaste woman should sit in the same room with'. Though their purity and chastity would protect them from seduction, they could still be contaminated by his perversity.

Dorian's final, Faustian attempt to redeem himself as he slides from corruption to crime (and it is the crime that betrays the corruption) is a conscious repetition of his relationship with Sibyl. Dorian meets a working-class village girl named Hetty who 'was quite beautiful and wonderfully like Sibyl Vane. I think it was that which first attracted me to her'. He plans to run off with her but decides, suddenly and at the last moment, 'to leave her as flower-like as I had found her'. Wotton reinforces the parallel with Sibyl by insisting that Dorian's noble sacrifice has in fact broken her heart and possibly caused her to kill herself. And he compares her to Ophelia and Perdita just as Dorian had compared Sibyl to Juliet and Rosalind. Wotton quite rightly denies the morality of Dorian's renunciation, and his worldly and sophisticated analysis destroys the last flicker of idealism in Dorian and confirms his damnation. Though Dorian is more deliberately cruel to Sibyl, he treats both Sibyl and Hetty in the same way, commits the terrible Victorian crime of toying with a young girl's affections and ruins their lives. The greatest similarity in these two unconsummated affairs is, of course, Dorian's attempt to use a pure woman to rescue himself from homosexuality. In both cases, when he is forced to commit himself emotionally and sexually to a woman, he becomes frightened, abandons her and returns to his old way of life.

In *De Profundis* (1905) Wilde writes that homosexual love 'was like feasting with panthers. The danger was half the excitement'. But the legal danger cut both ways and diminished the pleasure at the same time that it intensified the excitement. This double aspect of ecstasy and fear is reflected in the many polarities that create a vital tension in Dorian, who keenly felt 'the terrible pleasure of a double life': the man and the portrait, youth and age, beauty and ugliness, body and soul, freedom and conscience, life and art. This ambivalence is also manifested in Dorian's intense emotions which lead both to his crimes and to his almost anaesthetic lack of feeling about them, in his extreme variation between ruthless behaviour and guilty repentance, and in his simultaneous desire to conceal his actions and to confess them.

The overt moral of *Dorian Gray* is not convincing. It is too heavy-handed, obvious and *de rigueur*, and too inconsistent with the defiant tone of the novel, which delights in the Baudelairean fascination of sin and authorization of evil. For as T. S. Eliot writes of Baudelaire, 'The recognition of the reality of Sin is a New Life; and the possibility of damnation is itself . . . an immediate form of Salvation — of Salvation from the ennui of modern life, because it gives some significance to living.'[14]

Though Wilde insisted in his somewhat posturing Preface, 'There is no such thing as a moral or an immoral book', he felt obliged to emphasize the moral ending in his letters. He writes in 1890, the year the book was serialized, that Dorian Gray ('what I would like to be') 'is extremely impulsive, absurdly romantic, and is haunted all his life by an exaggerated sense of conscience which mars his pleasures for him . . . In his attempt to kill conscience, Dorian Gray kills himself.'[15] Though Dorian moves directly from renunciation of women to excess with men, Wilde's supposed 'moral is this: All excess as well as all renunciation brings its own punishment'.[16] Wilde begins by pleading for sexual freedom and ends by equating homosexuality with undefined and pervasive evil.

Dorian Gray is a failure as a novel because Wilde was unable to resolve the conflict between his desire for homosexual freedom and his fear of social condemnation. Though the picture represents Dorian's conscience, it would be more accurate to say (despite Wilde's statement) that he is haunted by the fear that the visual evidence of the picture will lead to the *discovery* of his crimes and his corruption. As long as he feels the painting is securely hidden, he does exactly as he pleases. But when he feels threatened by exposure, he becomes convinced that if he kills the painting with the same knife he used to kill the painter, 'It would kill the past, and when that was dead he would be free'. But Dorian is already as free as it is possible to be — in the Victorian age — for he has regressed to a state of childish and narcissistic irresponsibility. The aesthetic point of the novel may be that if instinct overcomes restraint, it will destroy art. But the real subject of the book, where 'conscience' stands for law and 'soul' for body, is the impossibility of achieving homosexual pleasure without the inevitable accompaniment of fear, guilt and self-hatred.

III

GIDE

The Immoralist

When the young Gide first met Wilde in Paris in 1891 he was fascinated by him and wrote that Wilde 'is always trying to instil into you a sanction for evil'.[1] Gide once again came under the influence of Wilde's dazzling conversation and heterodox ideas when the two writers met in January 1895, during Gide's second visit to Algeria, and his biographer George Painter claims that Wilde initiated Gide into homosexual pleasures.[2] The title of *The Immoralist* (1902) was probably suggested by the discussion of moral ambiguity in the Preface to *The Picture of Dorian Gray* (see the epigraph of the previous chapter), and Wilde appears in the novel as Ménalque, the victim of 'an absurd — a shameful — lawsuit [which] had caused a scandal and given the newspapers a convenient occasion to drag him through the mud'.[3]

Ménalque, a more serious, perceptive and self-controlled version of Lord Henry Wotton, also expresses himself in witty epigrams: 'I cannot expect everyone to have my virtues. It's good enough to meet with my vices.' Ménalque echoes Wotton's cynical justification of hedonism, diatribes against repression and defiant opposition to society, and he urges Michel to yield to temptation, realize his true nature and reach a new spirituality through sensuality:

> My only claim is to be natural, and the pleasure I feel in an action, I take as a sign that I ought to do it . . . Most [people] believe that it is only by constraint that they can get any good out of themselves, and so they live in a state of psychological distortion . . . The fear of finding oneself alone — that is what they suffer from — and so they don't find themselves at all . . . The part in each of us that we feel is different from other people is just the part that is rare, the part that makes our special value — and that is the very thing people try to suppress. (100)

The words 'psychological distortion', 'alone' and 'different' are metaphors for homosexuality; and Ménalque (unlike Wotton) represents an acceptable and even attractive image of the homosexual, for he is not a decadent aesthete but a traveller and an adventurer. He leads Michel toward self-awareness by telling him: 'instead of the learned man of habit you seemed to be in the old days, I know now that you are . . . [the ellipsis is in the text] it's for you to tell me what'. Ménalque's brief but crucial appearance in the novel provides a Wildean 'sanction for evil' and a reasoned alternative to conventional ideas about religion, marriage and the family. He encourages Michel's hedonism, justifies his apparently vicious and ruthless behaviour, and propels him on the way to 'immoralism', in the social as well as the sexual sense.[4]

In October 1895 (after meeting Wilde in Algeria just before his trials) Gide married his cousin Madeleine, but he never consummated the marriage with the woman who became his image of chaste spirituality. Painter explains that 'Gide's wife replaced his mother as a symbol of the pole of restraint and spiritual virtue to which he needed always to be able to return, and without which his other pole, of liberation, joy and perversion, would have lacked all meaning'.[5] The theme of *The Immoralist*, like that of *Dorian Gray*, is expressed through a series of conflicting polarities: morality and sensuality (not aestheticism, as in Wilde), sickness and health, intellect and body, asceticism and hedonism, altruism and egoism, Christianity and paganism. Michel's progress to immoralism is measured by his reaction against the first set of values and his movement toward their antitheses.

Some of the principal ideas of *The Immoralist* are foreshadowed in Gide's *Fruits of the Earth* (1897), which glorifies desire and instinct, and is a desperate attempt to free himself from his Puritan background.[6] Like Michel, who attempts to condemn and suppress everything that he owed to his past education and early moral beliefs, the autobiographical narrator of *Fruits of the Earth* says that 'I devoted three years of travel to forgetting all that I had learnt with my head . . . [and] found more instruction in pleasure than in books . . . [because] it is in pleasure that we become wholly conscious of ourselves'.[7] And like Dorian Gray under the tutelage of Henry Wotton, the narrator frees himself from repression and becomes an immoralist by abandoning himself to sensuality:

It was quite naturally that I had let myself go. I had of course heard it said that human nature was bad, but I wanted to put it to the proof . . . The secret workings of carnal desire drove me out of myself towards an enchanting confusion . . . For some time I had to consent to the abandonment of all moral considerations and cease resisting my desires . . .

I had succeeded in getting rid of all reticence and modesty, the reserves of decency, the hesitations of timidity — of all that makes pleasure fearful and predisposes the soul to remorse after the flagging of the flesh.[8]

The main difference between *Fruits of the Earth* and *The Immoralist* is that Gide is fulfilled by desire while Michel is dissatisfied by debauchery and finds pleasure like 'the manna of the desert which corrupts from one day to the next'.

The Immoralist portrays the unconscious repression and gradual revelation of Michel's homosexuality.[9] But his repression is so strong that he has to abandon his profession, destroy his marriage and suffer a nearly fatal disease before he is able to understand and accept the profound change in his life. Michel's progression to the role of immoralist is revealed in three ways: through a symmetrical series of sexual temptations, through the reversal of roles with his wife, and through his exposition and adoption of ideas that clearly derive from Nietzsche.

Michel's absorption in archeology and struggle against tuberculosis are both symbolic. Freud, who had a passion for archeology, explains that 'the psychoanalyst, like the archeologist in his excavations, must uncover layer after layer of the patient's psyche, before coming to the deepest, most valuable treasures'.[10] And Michel, when analysing his attempts to suppress his subconscious feelings, says, 'I compared myself to a palimpsest; I tasted the scholar's joy when he discovers under more recent writing, and on the same paper, a very ancient and infinitely more precious text' (51). On his farm in Normandy Michel listens to the voice of his past as it recalls the slightest details to his memory. When the great pond on his estate is drained, he explores his symbolic unconscious, sinks into the primeval ooze, finds creatures that lay on the bottom without ever coming up, and joins hands with his friend Charles (the son of his bailiff) to catch a large phallic eel.

As Michel begins to reject the past for the present and moves toward a more direct comprehension of life, he revises his ideas about history to match his new mode of existence. He is attracted to Athalaric, the young king of the Goths, whose rebellion against his Latin education and culture represents Michel's own tragic impulse toward a wilder and more natural state. Michel eulogizes 'nonculture' in his lectures on the Goths, and creates an elaborate analogy, expressed in the metaphor of disease, between the decline of later Latin civilization and his relationship with his wife, Marceline:

> I depicted artistic culture as welling up in a whole people, like a secretion, which is at first a sign of plethora, of a superabundance of health, but which afterwards stiffens, hardens, forbids the perfect contact of the mind with nature, hides under the persistent appearance of life a diminution of life, turns into an outside sheath, in which the cramped mind languishes and pines, in which at last it dies . . . I showed Culture, born of life, as the destroyer of life. (90)

The sexual meaning of this passage is unmistakable, and the welling up and stiffening that turns into a sheath and dies, suggests that Michel sees marital orgasm as a deathly process. For Michel, a learned Puritan who knew nothing of life and was totally absorbed in books and ruins, married Marceline without loving her in order to please his father. The betrothal took place at his father's deathbed, the wedding soon after his funeral, and the consummation — after several months of frigid gallantry — when Michel recovered from his grave attack of tuberculosis.

Michel's disease, which erupts after his marriage, symbolizes his homosexuality. It is secret and rather shameful, and (as Ménalque had suggested) sets him apart from other people. When Michel first spits blood into Marceline's handkerchief, he hides it from her but feels irritated when she fails to discover it. At the same time, however, the disease is liberating and life-enhancing, and his brush with death leads toward self-discovery and freedom. Most important, tuberculosis makes him introspective, forces him to change his ideas and way of life, and to set himself in opposition to the accepted values of society.

It is ironic that in an effort to aid his convalescence Marceline introduces Michel to a series of sexual temptations. For the Algerian setting liberates Michel's sensuality — 'a sort of ecstasy, of silent joy, of elation of the senses and the flesh' — at the same time that it allows and even encourages homosexual relations with handsome Arab boys.

Michel immediately notices that Bachir (the first of the boys) is naked under his patched burnous (later, when Michel is more aroused, he becomes more lyrical and sees 'a golden nudity beneath his floating garment'), and he soon establishes a 'blood tie' with the boy. Bachir cuts his thumb and licks his healthy wound like a complacent animal as the bright blood flows out. A few hours later Michel has his first haemorrhage and, like Zarathustra, can say, 'with my own blood I increased my own knowledge'.[11] Later in the novel Michel establishes another sympathetic bond with a mower on his farm in Normandy (this is one of several symmetrical incidents that link the two contrasting settings of the book). Though he is attracted to male blood, he is revolted by Marceline's bleeding after her miscarriage, her embolism and *her* haemorrhage. He subconsciously relates this unhealthy bleeding to her menstrual and hymeneal blood, and compares her to his stained possessions that are spoiled by the mark of death.

Moktir, another boy who soon becomes his favourite, offers a second temptation when Michel watches him steal Marceline's scissors and thrust them into the folds of his burnous. He is excited by this theft, allows himself to be robbed and enters into a secret conspiracy with the boy, who knows that Michel has seen him steal. This incident is also repeated on the farm when he encourages Alcide (Charles' brother) to continue poaching on his land after he catches him in an animal snare, wrestles with him and is pleasurably excited when Alcide is beaten for his own crime. Though these incidents show that Michel lacks a 'moral sense', their significance is primarily sexual. The scissors in the folds and the leg in the snare are symbols of copulation that reveal Michel's homosexual attraction and help to establish a male friendship. Michel abandons Bachir for Moktir just as he transfers his affections from Charles to Alcide (for Charles grows a beard after Michel has shaved his off).

Michel finds Marceline's presence awkward and undesirable when he is with the Arab boys and farm workers, and both conspiracies deliberately exclude her. Unlike his marriage, Michel's relationships with his servants entail no obligations and they can be dismissed when they become tiresome or inconvenient. Michel's dissimulation about his new self and the secret side of his life marks a significant step toward immoralism, and he soon discovers 'that the things that are reputed worst (lying, to mention only one [homosexuality would be another]) are only difficult to do as long as one has never done them; but that they become — and very quickly too — easy, pleasant, and agreeable to do over again, and soon even natural' (59).

Ménalque, whom Marceline instinctively dislikes, represents another temptation. He is a homosexual mentor who criticizes Michel's way of life and who lures him away from Marceline at a crucial moment of her difficult and dangerous pregnancy. When Michel returns home after 'abandoning' his wife to spend a final evening with Ménalque, he discovers that she has had the miscarriage that permanently damages her health and eventually leads to death.

On the farm in Normandy Michel is tempted not only by homosexual pleasures with Charles and Alcide, but also by the heterosexual perversions of incest and rape. He learns that the timber merchant Heurtevent, whose family is modelled on the Karamazovs, has had sexual relations with his daughter and that

> One night the eldest son had tried to rape a young servant girl, and as she struggled, the father had intervened to help his son and had held her with his huge hands, while the second son went piously on with his prayers on the floor above, and the youngest looked on at the drama as an amused spectator. (121)

Though Michel is fascinated by the lurid attractions of the Heurtevents, their bizarre activities merely intensify his revulsion from heterosexuality and increase his idealization of homosexuality.

Michel reveals his love for boys when he passes through Taormina on the way back to Biskra with the moribund Marceline and kisses the boy who drives them up the mountain to the hotel. The Sicilian youth is 'as beautiful as a line of Theocritus, full of colour, and odour and savour, like a fruit', and he recalls Michel's earlier visit to Syracuse when he 'reread Theocritus and reflected that his goatherds with the beautiful names were the very same as those I had loved at Biskra'. Gide used the beautiful name of Corydon, the *formusus pastor* of Virgil's *Eclogues*, as the title for his famous defence of homosexuality published in 1911. Michel's allusions to Theocritus are meant to justify homosexual love by relating it to life in ancient Greece where, according to Ménalque, 'ideas went hand in hand with life; so that the artist's life itself was already a poetic realization, the philosopher's life a putting into action of his philosophy; in this way, both philosophy and poetry took part in life' (106). As Gide writes more boldly in *Corydon*: 'It is remarkable that each renaissance or period of great activity, in whatever country it occurs, is always accompanied by a great outbreak of homosexuality'.[12]

The Theocritan kiss is closely related to an earlier scene with another coachman when Michel, having recovered from his illness, is travelling to Normandy with Marceline. He is waiting for her in Positano when her 'carriage, driven at a frantic pace, dashed suddenly into view'. Though the drunken driver has lost control of the carriage, he whips the frightened horse who suddenly collapses. Marceline jumps out of the carriage; and Michel wrestles with, beats and ties up the coachman, who tries to bite him (just as Alcide did when *they* wrestled together). That night, after several months of marriage, Michel sleeps with Marceline for the first time.

Unlike the other symbolic scenes in the novel, this one is entirely unconvincing. It is too contrived and too unrealistic: the sudden fall of the horse does not cause an accident; Marceline, who faints at the sight of blood, leaps out of the carriage; and Michel is uncommonly violent. On the literal level Michel, like a romantic hero, asserts his masculinity, protects his wife and earns his marital rights. His possession of Marceline is an egoistic assertion of his complete recovery and superior strength. On the allegorical level Michel, like his favourite Athalaric, flings 'aside his culture, as a restive horse shakes off a troublesome harness', for the scene reverses the platonic image of horses controlled by the charioteer and substitutes — to use Nietzche's terms — the Dionysian for the Apollonian element.

Both scenes use Plato's image of instinctual horses guided by a rational charioteer, but Gide makes the coachmen represent the hidden homosexual passion. In the Positano scene Michel sees the uncontrolled carriage taking his wife to destruction, represses his secret passion and makes love to her. In the Taormina scene his kiss, behind Marceline's back, symbolizes the indulgence of his secret passion. Whereas homosexuality was ugly, crude and uncontrolled in Positano, it becomes charming, literary and classical in Taormina.

Michel succumbs to the final temptations when he returns to Biskra. In Ravello, after his first trip to Algeria, he gazed into a pool of exquisitely pure and clear water, 'looked at himself for a long while — with no more shame now — with joy', and like Narcissus, fell in love with his own image. In Biskra he sees his negative image reflected in the Arab boys, for one explains that his marriage 'is a mere farce', and Michel (echoing Dorian Gray) asks himself: 'What fatigues, what vices, what sloth have put their ugly mark on faces that were once so bright with youth?' He insists that Moktir accompany them beyond Biskra to Touggourt and has vicarious sex with him by sharing Moktir's mistress. Just as he had discovered Marceline's miscarriage when he returned from his intellectual debauch with Ménalque, so he now finds her haemorrhaging when he returns from his physical debauch with Moktir. When his friends answer his summons and visit him in El Kantara, he is sleeping with Ali's sister, just as he had with Moktir's mistress, in order to keep the boy with him. And his sexual pleasure with this prostitute is increased by voyeurism when Ali surprises them in bed together.

Though Michel still maintains his last sordid contact with women, all his temptations — Bachir, Moktir, Charles, Ménalque, Alcide, the Theocritan coachboy and Ali — are homosexual, and all of them show his progressive estrangement from Marceline as he exchanges roles with her. On their first visit to Algeria Marceline's devoted nursing and passionate care save his life and restore his health, and his infantile dependence and sexual retardation are emphasized by the mother-son relationship. But when Michel discovers that he must free himself from Marceline before he can achieve self-realization, he rejects her prayers in order to avoid obligations to her — or even to God. When he first sleeps with his wife he infects her at the same time that he impregnates her. After that moment she declines as he improves, for her pregnancy leads to miscarriage and her tuberculosis to death.

Michel's cruelty to his wife and his sexual perversion are closely related, for his liberation depends on her death and she becomes the sacrificial victim for his sins: 'If she had said aloud, "Do you really care whether I live or not?" I should not have heard the words more clearly' (131). Though he has a horror of sympathy, 'the lurking place of every kind of contagion', he nurses her and pretends to love her while (like Dorian Gray), he sneaks off at night, indulges his 'shameless' appetites in debauches with the lowest dregs of society, and returns covered with vermin. His 'stubborn perseverance in evil', as the virtuous Marceline says, 'does away with the weak'; and though she is exhausted and crushed by the hostile landscape, he drives her past Biskra to Touggourt, where she loses her faith, has her final haemorrhage and dies stained with blood.

The profound influence of Nietzsche's thought on Gide is revealed in Michel's condemnation of traditional values, his sympathy with the strong, his desire to create a new morality out of sickness and pain, and his emphasis on the will as a means to transcend the self and achieve freedom. And Nietzsche's ideas distinguish the subtle and ironic *Immoralist* from the forced morality of *Dorian Gray* and the self-indulgent hedonism of *Fruits of the Earth*. Michel states the Nietzschean theme of the novel in the first paragraph of his narrative: 'To know how to free oneself is nothing; the arduous thing is to know what to do with one's freedom'. Ménalque echoes this idea when he tells Michel: 'The chief thing is to know what one wants'. But at the end of the novel Michel has not discovered what he wants, and though he has freed himself, he admits: 'This objectless liberty is a burden to me'. Before Marceline's death he observes that desire is sharpened by satisfaction; but after it he finds that 'Enjoyment here follows so closely upon desire that effort is impossible'. Michel's *will* to live, which was so strong when he was dying, is broken at the end of the novel when he lapses into Arab fatalism and becomes a pederast. The cyclical structure of the book and the repetition of symbolic incidents reflect Nietzsche's concept of eternal recurrence and emphasize the limitations rather than the possibilities of freedom. After all his liberating experiences, Michel is no better off at the end than he was at the beginning.

Michel's narrative is told to an audience of three bourgeois friends who are conventionally shocked but who still hope to bring him back into the fold of decent society. The kindly narrator's lack of perception emphasizes the abyss between Michel and himself, and at the end of the novel the audience becomes uneasy: 'We felt, alas, that by telling his story, Michel had made his action more legitimate'. Because they have not known at what point to condemn his story, they feel somewhat guilty themselves. Gide, who insists in the preface that the novel is not 'the exposition of a special case', uses the response of the audience not only as a contrast to Michel's character and spiritual adventure, but also to suggest that there are links between Michel and his friends and thus with ourselves.[13]

Michel's experiment with morality produces a state of mind as arid as the desert setting, for he is never able to integrate his ideas with his experience. He negates the platonic harmony of body and soul, instinct and reason, by disturbing the ancient order and traditional cultivation of his farm. He attempts to combine a Wildean defiance of society for the sake of pleasure with a Nietzschean emphasis on the gratification of the will. But the struggle to overcome his repression and to go beyond good and evil leaves him exhausted by pleasure and corrupted by a lack of self-knowledge. He ironically achieves a goal that proves illusory and his homosexual freedom, compounded of pleasure and guilt, remains profoundly ambiguous: 'a fruit filled with bitter ashes, like those colocynths of the desert that grow in a parched and burning soil. All they can offer to your thirst is a still more cruel fierceness — yet lying on the golden sand they are not without a beauty of their own' (7).

IV

MANN AND MUSIL

Death in Venice and *Young Törless*

He is old and his companion is young, yet he never leaves his side day or night if he can help it; he is driven on by an irresistible itch to the pleasures which are constantly to be found in seeing, hearing, and touching his beloved, in fact in every sensation which makes him conscious of his presence; no wonder then that he takes delight in close attendance on him.

Plato, *Phaedrus*

I

Death in Venice (1912), like *The Immoralist*, is strongly influenced by Nietzsche. The Apollonian-Dionysian polarity in *The Birth of Tragedy* (1871) is expressed in the opposition of culture, intellect, discipline, serenity and order to instinct, passion, licence, panic and chaos; of society to the individual, life to art, reality to illusion, health to sickness, perfection to decadence. Both Michel and Aschenbach move from the realm of abstract ideas to actual experience; and in the south, outside their own culture, find an instinctual release that leads to a fatal weakening of the will, to homosexuality, decadence, disease and destruction. Both novels question the repressive element in culture, and emphasize the classical wisdom of tempering the emotions with ethical restraint.

But Guerard's statement that both books present 'essentially the same story of a latent and unrecognized homosexuality leading to self-destruction'[1] is misleading, for the differences are perhaps more significant than the similarities. Gide's first-person confession is much more subjective and sympathetic to homosexuality than Mann's detached and ironic narrative. Michel condemns the old values, attempts to construct a new morality, maintains a hedonistic and self-consciously immoral attitude toward inversion and achieves

his liberation at the expense of Marceline. But in his powerful
Dostoyevskian novel, *The Abject,* Aschenbach renounced sympathy
with the abyss and 'taught a whole grateful generation that a man can
still be capable of moral resolution even after he has plumbed the
depths of knowledge'.[2] Though Aschenbach abandons his moral
resolution, he retains his asceticism and guilt, and pays for his
knowledge with his life. Whereas Michel seeks actual and physical
experience with the Arab boys, Aschenbach longs for the ideal and
the spiritual; and though he pursues Tadzio, he withdraws from any
direct contact which would ruin the purely aesthetic basis of their
relationship. As in Huysmans and Wilde, the homosexual theme in
Gide's *The Immoralist* is the *covert* but actual subject of the novel. And
though this theme is *overt* in *Death in Venice,* which carefully
describes the development of Aschenbach's homosexual passion, it
is not the real subject of the book. Mann employs homosexuality to
symbolize the core of passionate feeling that inspires great art, and
the theme of his novella is the possibility of self-destruction inherent
in creative genius.

The opening pages of Mann's novella brilliantly foreshadow the
theme of death by cholera in Venice, a sinking city whose history of
sensual self-indulgence had led to a moral decline and physical
collapse. The first of three symbolic messengers of death, a distinctly
exotic figure with straw hat, red hair, snub nose, prominent Adam's
apple and glistening white teeth laid bare to the gums, suddenly
appears in the Byzantine-style mortuary chapel — a parody of St
Mark's basilica — opposite the North Cemetery in Munich. This
disturbing apparition weakens Aschenbach's repressive self-control,
inspires 'a widening of inward barriers, a kind of vaulting unrest, a
youthfully ardent search for distant scenes'. It also stimulates his
visionary dream which represents the source of the Asiatic cholera in
the moist swamps of the Ganges delta as well as his own unconscious
psyche: 'He beheld a landscape, a tropical marshland, beneath a
reeking sky, steaming, monstrous, rank — a kind of primeval
wilderness of islands, morasses, and alluvial channels . . . Among the
knotted joints of a bamboo thicket the eyes of a crouching tiger
gleamed — and he felt his heart throb with terror, yet with a longing
inexplicable' (5-6). This unexpected 'contagion' of travel intensifies
the conflict between Aschenbach's rigid German routine of cold and

passionate service and his Mediterranean craving for freedom, release, forgetfulness; between the closed fist and the open hand; between 'Hold fast', the motto of his hero Frederick the Great (who was a homosexual) and the growing fatigue and enervation of the will.

This crucial contrast is expressed in the figure of St Sebastian, who exemplifies Aschenbach's typical hero and represents 'an intellectual and virginal manliness, which clenches its teeth and stands in modest defiance of the swords and spears that pierce its side . . . The figure of Sebastian is the most beautiful symbol, if not of art as a whole, yet certainly of the art we speak of here' (11). Mann exploits the homosexual connotations in the iconography of St Sebastian, a beautiful, well-formed but helpless youth who is either dreamily indifferent to or masochistically ecstatic about the *arrows* (not as Mann suggests with some exaggeration, the swords and spears) that penetrate his thinly-clad and bloody body[3]. And he uses the image of the passive martyr, who also manifests the weakness inherent in Aschenbach's work, to pre-figure Tadzio, and to suggest the ambiguous relation of art and morality, of creative genius and self-destruction.

Aschenbach's art celebrates the 'heroism born of weakness', makes a virtue out of the very attempt to create and projects his ideal of 'forbearance in the face of fate' through characters who endure psychological strain with dignity. Aschenbach himself derives his dignity from 'pride in the word', the awareness that by sacrificing his life to art he has achieved mastery over 'the disintegrating effect of knowledge' and the abyss of human behaviour, over the passions and mysteries of the subconscious that have been explored by modern thinkers and are no longer held in check by moral or religious traditions.

Yet, the narrator of the novella comments, there are weaknesses inherent in Aschenbach's hard-won and confident belief that he has subdued knowledge and feeling in the pursuit of form. First, his very success leads him to the dangerous assumption that the control he has achieved in art will also enable him to control his life. He is vulnerable to the evils of the world because he feels he has mastered them. Secondly, Aschenbach has totally committed himself to form — the pursuit of artistic perfection. But form is both moral, as Aschenbach thinks, since it is the expression and result of discipline, and also immoral '— yes, actually hostile to morality — in that of its very essence it is indifferent to good and evil, and deliberately concerned to make the moral world stoop beneath its proud and undivided sceptre' (14). In this crucial qualification of Aschenbach's beliefs the narrator suggests that no one can attribute moral values to pure form, which is not necessarily and intrinsically good, and states that its indifference to morality mocks the artist's efforts to create an ordered moral world.

Aschenbach justifies the agony of his creative genius — and anticipates the collapse of his discipline and abandonment of moral values — by a belief in 'the idea that almost everything conspicuously great is great in despite: has come into being in defiance of affliction and pain, poverty, destitution, bodily weakness, vice and passion' (11). By contrast, Tadzio achieves his inspiring 'perfection of form' naturally and effortlessly — like a god. Aschenbach's homosexual passion teaches him that he cannot control his own fate, indeed cannot even save his own life in the face of overwhelming emotion. Tadzio, the love-object, links art with death, and becomes at once the symbol of perfect form that eludes the artist and the rigidly repressed passion that destroys him.

This thematic prelude and the revealing sketch of Aschenbach's character establish the intellectual framework of the novella, suggest the inevitability of his tragic fate, and lead to a series of encounters with menacing and vaguely theatrical figures. The goat-bearded 'circus director' (attended by a hunch-backed sailor) sells Aschenbach the ticket across the northern Adriatic from Pola to Venice and seals their satanic pact with the sand which, like that in his parents' hour-glass, warns of human mortality. The aged and grotesque homosexual with dyed hair, rouged cheeks and false teeth cavorts with the youths on the ship and with his tongue makes 'a suggestive motion ugly to behold'. And Charon, the second messenger of death, complete with straw hat, snub nose and white teeth bared to the gums, conveys Aschenbach, against his will, from the dock to the Lido in a coffin-like gondola, and then suddenly vanishes after the cryptic warning: 'The signore will pay'.

When Aschenbach encounters Tadzio's perfect beauty, delightful charm and expression of pure serenity he does not see him as an actual boy of fourteen, but as an embodiment of Greek art, transmuted and gilded with mythical significance. Aschenbach alludes to Homer, Xenophon and Ovid, and constantly compares the golden-haired youth to Greek sculpture in Parian marble, to Cleitos, Cephalus, Orion, Hyacinthus and, of course, to Narcissus. The classical allusions not only idealize Tadzio but also foreshadow his doom, for all these beautiful Greeks were destroyed by passion. Aschenbach sees Tadzio, as Hallward saw Dorian Gray, as 'the visible incarnation of that unseen ideal'[4] which he hopes to re-create in his own art. His classical idealization of Tadzio, the mirror and image of spiritual beauty whose mellifluous name sounds like the musical syllables of *adagio*,[5] is partly the instinctive habit of the scholar who encounters beauty in a Mediterranean country, partly an expression of his aesthetic taste and partly a defence against his own surging feelings.

The old and ugly Aschenbach imagines his adoration of Tadzio — whose passive response seems to be motivated by adolescent flirtatiousness, vanity and narcissism — as the modern equivalent of Socrates' love for Phaedrus, though Plato does not suggest, in the actual *Phaedrus,* that Socrates is wooing the youth. Aschenbach renounces Socrates' insinuating wit and charming turns of phrase, and seduces Tadzio with meaningful glances that seek and meet the eye of the beloved. Tadzio sees 'himself in his lover as in a glass',[6] and his responsive looks lead Aschenbach to address the boy in his imagination. Though Aschenbach is dominated by passion, he attempts to express — and therefore to control — this passion by means of his intellect, and he represents his feelings as a platonic search for the good. But his paraphrase of Plato merely emphasizes his tragic dilemma and forms an ironic counterpart to his absurd degeneration.

Like Socrates — who was forced to commit suicide for corrupting the youth of Athens — Aschenbach, under the influence of Tadzio, now equates beauty with goodness, and stresses the moral and spiritual qualities of perfect form. Plato writes that the lover

> who has had a full sight of the celestial vision, when he beholds a god-like face or a physical form which truly reflects ideal beauty, first of all shivers and experiences something of the dread which the vision itself inspired; next he gazes upon it and worships it as if it were a god, and, if he were not afraid of being thought an utter madman, he would sacrifice to his beloved as to the image of a

divinity . . . Beauty shone bright in the world above, and here too it gleams clearest, even as the sense by which we apprehend it is our clearest.[7]

This is how the lover makes the transition from beauty on earth to absolute beauty. Aschenbach, who imaginatively communicates with Tadzio on an ideal plane, also experiences

> the fear and reverence felt by the noble soul when he beholds a godlike face or a form which is the good image of beauty: how as he gazes he worships the beautiful one and scarcely dares to look upon him, but would offer sacrifice as to an idol or a god, did he not fear to be thought stark mad. 'For beauty, my Phaedrus, beauty alone, is lovely and visible at once. For, mark you, it is the sole aspect of the spiritual which we can perceive through our senses . . . So beauty, then, is the beauty-lover's way to the spirit.'
> (48)

The irony of Aschenbach's futile attempt to idealize his pederastic passion and substitute Elysium for Hades is emphasized by the parallel development of his love and the progress of the cholera that insidiously infects the city.[8] For Aschenbach, the highly respectable widower with one married daughter (he has no son, just as Tadzio seems to have no father), changes from a passive to an active lover, from a purely intellectual and aesthetic admirer of Tadzio's beauty to a man who suddenly realizes that the acute pain he felt during his quite sensible attempt to leave the city (fortuitously prevented by the loss of his trunk) was due entirely to his rapturous though unacknowledged feeling for the youth. His half-hearted attempt to speak to the boy,[9] join body and mind, and effect a sane recovery from his folly fails. Aschenbach's imaginative possession of Tadzio is more intense and more meaningful than physical possession, and he does not want to exchange illusion for reality.

After he whispers the confession of love to himself he throws off the final restraints. The writer whose sternly moral works were adopted as school textbooks is now driven to degeneration by his mania, and openly pursues the boy through the narrow and unclean passages of the town: 'drunk with passion, his footsteps [were] guided by the daemonic power whose pastime it is to trample on human reason and dignity . . . His frenzy left him capacity for nothing else but to pursue his flame', and he remained 'powerless to tear himself away, blind to the danger of being caught in so mad an attitude' (58-9).[10]

Aschenbach's passion is like a crime, and the city's evil secret of the cholera (whose deadly convulsions parody the sexual climax) mingles with the one in the depths of his heart. As Mann writes in 'Goethe and Tolstoy': 'Disease has two faces and a double relation to man and his human dignity. On the one hand it is hostile: by overstressing the physical, by throwing man back upon his own body, it has a dehumanizing effect. On the other hand, it is possible to think and feel about illness as a highly dignified human phenomenon.'[11] A sanitary inspector greets Aschenbach's ship as it approaches Venice, the lukewarm air of the sirocco breathes on him as he is rowed to the Lido, he smells the stagnant odour of the lagoon when he opens his hotel window, the sickening exhalations of the canals nearly drive him from the city, and the pungent smell of carbolic acid and municipal placards warn him of the danger of certain intestinal infections. The ominous reports in the German newspapers, which explain the disappearance of his countrymen, are confirmed by the blustering, equivocal street musician, the third messenger of death, who laconically confides that the sirocco is oppressive and 'Not good for the health'. And even when the English clerk in Cook's describes the source of the cholera on the mephitic banks of the Ganges (which recalls Aschenbach's first dream in Munich) and advises him to leave immediately in order to avoid the imminent blockade, he cannot tear himself away from the grip of the pestilence. The nearness of his beloved holds him in a spell and he is absolutely unable to stir.

When Aschenbach learns he is in mortal danger, he realizes that the 'one decent, expiatory course' open to him is to warn Tadzio's mother and urge her to flee at once. Though this advice would save their lives and restore his self-possession, Aschenbach decides to join the conspiracy and hide the guilty knowledge. His irrational and even sinister behaviour is explained not only by his fear of losing Tadzio and desire to be quarantined with him in the abandoned city, but also by his early response to Tadzio's imperfect teeth: ' "He is delicate, he is sickly," Aschenbach thought. "He will most likely not live to grow old." He did not try to account for the pleasure the idea gave him' (36).

Tadzio's poor teeth connect him with the aged homosexual on the ship, and this symbol of his anaemic disease and human mortality is pleasurable to Aschenbach because it equalizes youth and age, beauty and ugliness, and diminishes Tadzio's godlike power over him. The writer is possessively jealous of the youth's perfect form, and wants him to die at the height of his beauty, before he is ravaged by decay and old age. He includes Tadzio in his own wish for death, the final release; and the boy's death seems appropriate to Aschenbach, who associates art with disease and suffering.

The actual, as opposed to the idealized meaning of Aschenbach's Socratic 'sacrifice as to an idol or a god' is revealed in the dream that occurs immediately after he discovers the full implications of the cholera and refuses to warn the Polish family about it. This disturbing vision is a powerful contrast to the Apollonian order and reason of the Socratic dialogue and of the 'primeval legend, handed down from the beginning of time, of the birth of form', for it expresses his unconscious fears and desires, and ravages the cultural foundations of his life. As his will disintegrates amidst the stench of wounds, uncleanliness and disease, Aschenbach 'craved with all his soul to join the ring that formed about the obscene symbol [the phallus] of the godhead'. He finally gives himself up to the Dionysian 'orgy of promiscuous embraces — and in his very soul tasted the bestial degradation of his fall' (72). This terrifying dream denies the relationship of beauty, love and moral goodness, and suggests that Aschenbach's long-sought release is totally negative and destructive: 'it seemed to him as though the moral law were fallen in ruins and only the monstrous and the perverse held out a hope' (73).

Overwhelmed by passion and disgusted by his ageing body, Aschenbach submits to the cosmetic attentions of the hotel barber, who transforms him into a grotesque replica of the repulsive old invert on the ship. The theatrical make-up is not only a visible manifestation of Aschenbach's corruption, but also an ironic comment on his search for true beauty, for in the *Phaedrus* the effeminate boy also supplies 'his natural deficiency of complexion by use of cosmetics'.[12] Aschenbach, however, is delighted by his sudden rejuvenation, and he pursues Tadzio into Venice wearing a red tie and straw hat which link him to the boy's red-silk breast knot and to the hats of the messengers of death. But he is soon exhausted by his unsuccessful search; and in the little square where he had once conceived the plan of his abortive flight, he eats the over-ripe strawberries that infect him with the fatal cholera, and once again thinks of Socrates' dialogue with Phaedrus.

Socrates makes two speeches in the *Phaedrus*. In the first he maintains, in opposition to Lysias, that sensual love is merely the irrational desire for the enjoyment of physical beauty. But Socrates' second speech is a palinode or recantation of the first. In the later speech he states that love is the link between the world of the senses and the world of Forms, and prompts the soul to recapture the vision of the ideal world. Aschenbach's first Socratic speech faithfully paraphrases Socrates' *second* speech, which glorifies love. But Aschenbach's second speech, though presented in a Socratic guise, is 'shaped in his disordered brain by the fantastic logic that governs our dreams', and is an imaginative exaggeration of the idea of Socrates' *first* — and negative — speech. Thus Aschenbach's final statement, based on his own degraded position and his absolute failure 'to grow wings and endeavour to fly upwards' to true beauty, is diametrically opposed to Socrates' final statement and arrives at the conclusion that Plato rejects. Socrates connects beauty with knowledge, while Aschenbach denies platonic idealism and sees beauty and knowledge as two different paths to the abyss.

In his second 'platonic' speech Aschenbach, who speaks as an artist and not as a philosopher, begins by quoting Socrates' statement that beauty is the sole aspect of the spiritual that we can perceive through our senses. But Aschenbach then warns his imaginary Phaedrus that it is dangerous to attempt to reach the spirit through this perilous path, and expresses disillusionment with his reputation and with the course of his career. For, he states, poets need Eros as their companion and guide and, like women, are prone to excess and tend to lose themselves in the realm of feeling. Their style, fame and moral authority are spurious since they reject the knowledge that might destroy them. 'For knowledge, Phaedrus, does not make him who possesses it dignified or austere. Knowledge is all-knowing, understanding, forgiving; it takes up no position, sets no store by form. It has compassion with the abyss — it *is* the abyss' (77). Because this self-knowledge, especially an understanding of the repressed and therefore more dangerous aspects of the personality, tends to strengthen the hold of the evil, the forbidden and the ethically impossible, poets renounce such knowledge for beauty. But, Aschenbach continues, detachment and 'preoccupation with form [also] lead to intoxication and desire, they may lead the noblest among us to frightful emotional excesses, which his own stern cult of the beautiful would make him the first to condemn. So they too, they too, lead to the bottomless pit' (77). Aschenbach's pathetic personal example and his perversion of Socratic thought suggest that the poet is doomed by the very qualities that account for his creative power, whether he follows the path of knowledge or of beauty. For the artist 'whose sole preoccupation is with excellence longs fervently to find rest in perfection; and is not nothingness a form of perfection?' (32).

The doomed Aschenbach then returns to the hotel to discover that Tadzio is leaving. When he rushes to the beach for a final glimpse of the beautiful boy he finds that Tadzio's friend Jaschiu — who once kissed the beloved while Aschenbach compensated himself with 'luscious dead-ripe' strawberries — is avenging himself for his long weeks of subserviency to Tadzio, of stooping (like Aschenbach) beneath his proud sceptre. Jaschiu challenges Tadzio to a fight and presses his 'face into the sand — for so long a time that it seemed the exhausted lad might even suffocate. He made spasmodic efforts to shake the other off, lay still and then began a feeble twitching' (78). This scene symbolizes the degradation of beauty and form, and at the same time, the spiritual forbearance in the face of fate and constancy of beauty under torture that was represented in the figure of St Sebastian, who 'was specially invoked as a patron against the plague'.[13] After witnessing this scene, the artist is 'summoned' by Tadzio, the final messenger of death.

Though the conclusion of *Death in Venice* is ambiguous, it is difficult to agree with Trilling's statement that 'If Mann's Aschenbach dies at the height of his intellectual and artistic powers, overcome by a passion that his ethical reason condemns, we do not take this to be a defeat, rather a kind of terrible rebirth: at his latter end the artist knows a reality that he had until now refused to admit to consciousness'.[14] For Aschenbach does not die at the height of his artistic powers, but expires in a state of profound degeneration as 'the rouged and flabby mouth uttered single words of the sentences shaped in his disordered brain' (76). Though Aschenbach thought that the figure of Tadzio would be the divine model for his style,[15] that masterpiece of nature never inspires Aschenbach's creative genius nor breaks the artistic impasse that forced him to leave Munich. The only thing he writes in Venice is a page and a half of mannered and decadent prose that barely conceals the dry rot of its intellectual foundations. The thoroughly ironic mode of the novella and Aschenbach's premature death suggest that though he knows a new reality at the end of his life, this self-knowledge cannot be transformed into art: 'It has compassion with the abyss — it *is* the abyss'.

Mann makes Aschenbach a homosexual for several reasons. On one level homosexuality is a manifestation of strain and disorder, a release of psychological repression that results in the vulgar and degrading passion of an elderly gentleman for a rather cruel and unworthy boy. Aschenbach abandons his will, conspires with pseudo-artists like the equivocal musician and the cosmetic barber, sadly deludes himself about his relationship to Tadzio, and condemns himself — and probably his beloved — to death.

More importantly, Aschenbach's homosexual pursuit is symbolic of the artist's noble but tragic quest for perfection. In *Phaedrus* Socrates concludes that the lover who does not seek mere sensual gratification is the one who truly serves the god of love since the contemplation of beauty is more important than the pleasure of the moment, which is lost as soon as it is gratified. Mann adapts this idea to his theme when he makes Aschenbach, who fails to ascend from Tadzio's physical beauty to a higher ideal form, die in a kind of Wagnerian *Liebestod* while contemplating perfect beauty.

Mann's imaginative artist, who paradoxically creates in his work a life that he is unable to live in reality, must maintain a subtle and perilous balance of feeling and thought, and cannot surrender to either without losing his capacity to write. Aschenbach's first dream in Munich reveals the existence of his passionate though repressed feelings, which contribute to the greatness of his art as long as they are controlled by the discipline and restraint of 'the poet-spokesman of all those who labour at the edge of exhaustion; of [those] . . . who yet contrive by skilful husbanding and prodigious spasms of will to produce, at least for a while, the effect of greatness' (12). Repression is, paradoxically, vital for expression; and without Apollonian form, Aschenbach's Dionysian passion becomes wild and useless, like that of the other artist-types in Mann's stories: Spinell in 'Tristan',

Siegmund in 'The Blood of the Walsungs' and Cipolla in 'Mario and the Magician'. And yet, as Plato writes: 'If a man comes to the door of poetry untouched by the madness of the Muses, believing that technique alone will make him a good poet, he and his compositions will never reach perfection, but are utterly eclipsed by the performances of the inspired madman'.[16] In the doomed love of the suspect and anti-social pederast, Mann found the perfect pattern for the artist's desperate struggle to recapture the ideal form of sensual beauty, and to unite passion with thought, grace with wisdom, the real with the ideal.

II

Young Törless (1906), by Mann's contemporary Robert Musil, is an interesting contrast to *Death in Venice* and provides a useful transition to *Cities of the Plain* and *Seven Pillars of Wisdom*. Wilde, Gide and Mann are all concerned with the aesthetic and idealistic aspects of homosexuality, though they frequently express them through their moral complements: decadence and guilt. But in Musil, who is more realistic in his description of inversion than practising homosexuals, there is no platonic transfiguration of the theme, no exotic culture, no ambiguity, no apologetics, no sympathy. His book is spare, harsh, brutal, arid and thoroughly negative.

In Mann's allegory of Fascism, Cipolla (Mussolini) hypnotizes Mario and forces the handsome young waiter to kiss him, and this homosexual submission symbolizes man's degradation under the tyranny of force. And in *Doctor Faustus*, the homosexual element in the friendship of Rudi and Adrian is one manifestation of the satanic evil of Nazism. In a similar way, Musil uses the sado-masochistic aspect of inversion, which fills the moral vacuum at a boys' school, to emphasize the cruelty of power. Though icily objective, *Young Törless* prepares us for the painful and perceptive self-scrutiny of Proust and T. E. Lawrence.

In *Young Törless* Musil portrays the inner life of a sensitive adolescent at a crucial moment of his psychological development and describes his brutalizing experience with homosexuality. Musil imposes severe limitations on his extremely abstract and cerebral book, and achieves concentration, intensity and power at the expense of character and plot, the traditional concerns of the novel.

For there is virtually no description of the physical setting or the life of the school, the parents and teachers are left deliberately vague, the whore is a cliché, and even the boys have an unusual taste for theoretical mathematics, philosophical speculation and metaphorical language.

The élite military academy on the desolate Polish frontier of the Austro-Hungarian Empire is based on the school at Mahrisch-Weisskirchen in Moravia that Musil (and Rilke) attended during 1894-7. Though it is meant 'to safeguard the young generation, in its years of awakening, from the corrupting influences of a large city',[17] the school, which represents the rot of an Empire in the last stages of decay, breeds its own form of corruption. The three main influences on the boys — their parents, the church and the army — all become perverted behind the grey institutional walls.

As the novel opens Törless, younger and smaller than the other boys, is a protected mother's darling who 'had had a quite unspeakable yearning to be a little girl'. When he says farewell to his mother at the railroad station of the school he suffers from agonizing homesickness, egoistic gloom and morbid introspection. But during the 'larval period' of his life that is recorded in the novel Törless gradually severs the psychological dependence on his mother, and when she finally returns to take him home he has lost most of his feeling for her.

Törless' 'peculiar kind of sensuality was more deeply hidden, more forceful, and of a darker hue than that of his friends, and more slow and difficult in its manifestations' (23), and these feelings are expressed through love for his mother, degradation with the village whore Božena, and passion for his classmate Basini. When he visits Božena, with his 'dainty sword' symbolically dangling from his side, he is unable to forget his mother and realizes that the two women are inextricably linked in his mind. Božena displays her crudest and most repellent qualities in order to attract Törless; and in an effort to achieve sexual freedom he betrays the image of his mother and deliberately descends lower than the common people until he feels like a small, unclean animal. The adolescent longing for an idealized woman results in monstrous lust and abounding humiliations; and 'the awakening boy's first passion is not love for the one, but hatred for all' — especially himself.

Törless' profanation of his mother leads to a loss of 'spiritual force' and a gradual identification with the sadistic and bloody religious images — the writhing flagellants and martyrs' deaths — that surround him in the Catholic school. As he suppresses the more sensitive female element within himself, he adopts the rough brutality of his older friends. Though he develops a brief friendship with the effeminate Prince H., which (though not described) is called 'subtle and full of rare fascination', the conflict between his pure and coarse modes of experience forces him to attack the Prince's religious beliefs and to destroy their friendship.

The essence of the novel, Törless' relationship with the unfortunate Basini, who is caught stealing and subjected to torture by Törless' companions, Reiting and Beineberg (whose big ears stick out like his sword), is closely related to all the major themes: political, maternal, military, religious and sexual. Both Božena and Basini, who represent the Slavic and Italian minorities who are dominated by the Austrians, are contrasted to the Germanic ethos of Törless and his friends, and compared to each other. For the coquettish and physically underdeveloped Basini attempts to compensate for his inadequacies by 'playing the man' with Božena, though he never actually sleeps with her. Törless finds in Basini a surrogate for Prince H. as well as a beautiful compensation for the squalor he had been blighted with, in the depths of his loneliness, by his experience with Božena. When Basini is interrogated about his theft he is like a little animal, just as Törless had been with Božena; and when he is beaten and covered with weals, 'his movements were as wretched as those of a clumsy prostitute'.

Like the army, the cloistered atmosphere of the school provides no acceptable outlet for the boys' sexual desires — 'seething, passionate, naked and loaded with destruction' — and they are inevitably forced into whoring and homosexuality. Basini, who is both weak and effeminate, with 'a chaste, slender willingness, like that of a young girl', is the perfect sexual victim. His weakness stimulates the sadistic impulses that spring from repressed sexuality and from the military ethos of brutality and power. Basini, who provides the same fascination as a naked woman, becomes the personification of the flagellants and martyrs when he is tortured and bloody. His 'sacrifice' is supposed to have a 'purifying effect', but his religious passion aggravates the torturers' sexual guilt at the same time that it stimulates their sexual excitement.

The fact that Basini is guilty of a crime allows Reiting and
Beineberg to justify his humiliation on moral grounds and to punish
him for their own sexual offences; and his interrogation soon leads to
torture and to homosexuality. The boys' hatred is unleashed on the
degraded yet pliant Basini, a 'rotten swine' who has forfeited his
right to exist, in a secret, concealed room behind a locked door that is
approached by a narrow tunnel and smells of unopened trunks — an
obvious symbol for the unconscious.

At first Törless is merely an observer who is perplexed and
uncomfortable about his passive relation to the suffering Basini and
puzzled by the 'queer fascination' that the boy holds for him. This
fascination is clarified when Törless realizes that, like Reiting and
Beineberg, he is sexually aroused by Basini's suffering. Törless
makes an unsuccessful attempt to discover an answer to his
perplexities through the study of mathematics and philosophy, and
an unrewarding discussion with his teacher. But the real illumina-
tion comes when Basini confesses his homosexual relations with
Reiting and Beineberg, and seeks the friendship of Törless, mainly
for protection and partly because he desperately needs the love of a
kindred spirit:

> In the next instant, with crazy speed, Basini flung off his
> nightclothes and slid under the blankets and was pressing his
> naked, trembling body against Törless . . .
> Lust, which had been slowly seeping into him, emanating from
> every single moment of desperation, had now grown to its full
> stature. It lay naked at his side and covered his head with its soft
> black cloak. (142-3)

Despite his characteristic use of an abstraction, Lust, to express
emotion, Musil is unusually frank about homosexuality, which is
manifested in sadism and symbolizes perverted power.

Törless has cultivated an ability to 'see things in two different
ways' and is 'torn between two worlds': the everyday world of
respectable citizens (like his parents) and the other world of
darkness, mystery and blood (his school). He is both revolted and
fascinated by 'the various little vices that boys went in for', yet
oscillates between agony and rapture, shame and desire, lucidity and
illusion. He feels tenderness for Basini at the same time that he
despises him, and realizes that Basini is merely 'a provisional object

of his longing': 'although Törless did debase himself with him, his desire was never satisfied by him; on the contrary, it went growing out beyond Basini, into some new and aimless craving'. But the degrading element in his relationship with Basini has left a 'toxic substance' behind which is needed to give the soul 'a sort of health that is more acute, and subtler, and wiser'. This is the wisdom acquired from the experience of evil which, Musil suggests, is necessary to growth and to life.

When Törless learns that he is being used by Basini as a means of escape from his tormentors, his feelings turn to straightforward repugnance. He now wants to become defiled — and thus freed — by his vicarious participation in Basini's humiliation, just as he had hoped to free himself from his mother through Božena. The communal beating of Basini, incited by Reiting and Beineberg, shows how their sadism has spread throughout the school; though it seems incredible that the shadowy teachers, however obtuse, could be totally unaware of what is happening.

The conclusion of this disturbing novel is negative and rather cynical. Basini, unable to endure further torture, gives himself up, is condemned by the school and expelled. Törless, morally and aesthetically disgusted by the treatment of Basini, runs away, is brought back and tries to explain his feelings to the teachers. Musil attempts to describe all the experience of the novel in terms of Törless' feelings, but his 'new and aimless craving' and 'flood of dark stirrings' are never defined. The hopelessly baffled teachers, who reaffirm the banality of evil by passively accepting it, suggest that Törless leave the school to be educated privately. He returns home radically changed and alienated from his mother, but we never learn precisely how his experience has affected his character and his life. Reiting, Beineberg and the evil symbolized by the homosexual rites in the secret attic remain untouched and entrenched. Though it is tempting to read retrospective meaning into the novel, after the horrors of German militarism in the two world wars, the homosexual theme of *Young Törless* is not strong enough to bear the allegorical implications which, unlike those of Musil's major work, *The Man Without Qualities,* are sounded but not developed.

V

PROUST

Cities of the Plain

I

Homosexuality dominated Proust's life as well as his art, and his sexual descent from idealism to degradation is reflected in the dramatic degeneration of his fictional characters. Despite his bravado with Gide, he felt guilty about his homosexuality and frustrated in his love for young boys, and Painter writes of Proust in 1917:

> His vice had begun with love for his equals (Reynaldo Hahn and Lucien Daudet), progressed through platonic affection for social superiors (Fénelon, Antoine Bibesco, and the rest) to physical affection for social inferiors (Ulrich and Agostinelli), and now ended, disillusioned with all, in a sterile intercourse with professional catamites. He was experimenting with evil . . . and testing his power to associate with it unscathed. He was buying cheaply, for money and without expense of time or emotion, not only pleasure but human society, albeit in its basest form.[1]

The symbolic good-night kiss in the Overture to *Swann's Way* makes it clear that Proust's mother determined his sexual as well as his artistic nature, for the much-desired kiss — withheld at first by the command of his father and then indulgently surrendered — symbolizes the nourishing but destructive love that prevented him from loving another woman. Proust's mother represented a touchstone of goodness, a kind of living conscience, and her death in 1905 marked a crucial turning point in her son's emotional life. For Proust, whom Gide called 'that great master of dissimulation',[2] had no further need to disguise and restrain his inversion. As he writes in *Cities of the Plain*, generalizing from his own experience, homosexuals are 'sons without a mother, to whom they are obliged to lie all her life long and even in the hour when they close her dying eyes'.[3] This richly suggestive sentence implies that even Proust, who had enjoyed maternal love and devotion, was in a vital sense 'without a mother', and that his sense of unworthiness and guilt about the rejection of her values and the betrayal of her love was related to his subconscious wish for her death.

Like Baudelaire, Proust believed that one of the principal pleasures of love was the knowledge of doing evil. The profound conflict between his filial love and desire to indulge his sado-masochistic urges led him to profane his mother by connecting her with male prostitutes. In the spring of 1917 Proust gave Albert LeCuziat, footman of the Duc de Rohan and model for the character of Jupien, the necessary financial assistance to open a male brothel and furnished this smart establishment with the second-best but solidly bourgeois chairs, sofas and carpets of his dead parents. Proust took a more than proprietary interest in the brothel he had endowed, and sometimes achieved sexual satisfaction by desecrating his mother's photograph in front of his lovers.

The profanation theme pervades Proust's novel, and he writes that 'sons, who do not always take after their fathers, even without being inverts, and though they go after women, may consummate upon their faces the profanation of their mothers. But we need not consider here a subject that deserves a chapter to itself: the Profanation of the Mother' (ii.75). Proust's suggestion that a son's effeminate expression may betray his sexual tastes and that heterosexual union is a symbolic displacement of the son's incestuous desire for the mother helps to explain his homosexuality. As Gide observes, the Greek fable 'teaches us that Achilles was invulnerable except in that spot of his body which had been made soft by the remembrance of his mother's touch'.[4]

Unlike many homosexual writers Proust does not regard himself as superior to the female sex, nor look down upon women, nor, with a kind of apostolic zeal, make homosexuality the privilege of great genius and glorious epochs of history. And he does not claim exemption, as an artist, from all norms of moral behaviour and social responsibility. On the contrary, he is quite frank about the desperately unhappy love affairs that made him suffer at the same time that they inspired him to portray sexual suffering. All the love affairs in the novel thrive on deception, jealousy and pain, lead to emotional upheavals, and have the effect of a strange aberration or an incurable malady. Proust's dissection and condemnation of homosexuality, an exorcism as well as a narrative, is at once an expression of guilt, a means to self-knowledge and an attempt to control his emotions by ordering them in art. His novel demonstrates the truth of D. H. Lawrence's belief that 'One sheds one's sicknesses in books — repeats and presents again one's emotions, to be master of them'.[5]

Proust's Introduction to *Cities of the Plain* (1921-2), the volume of *Remembrance of Things Past* that is most directly concerned with the inversion of Albertine, Charlus and Morel, considers the modern descendants of the inhabitants of Sodom. It is a remarkable *tour de force* that analyses the psychology of homosexuals and their role in society, and provides an intellectual and emotional framework for judging the characters and events of the novel. The sexual encounter between Charlus and Jupien and the extensive discussion that follows it form the basis of our understanding of Charlus' character and subsequent development, constitute a vital stage in Marcel's growth and awareness, and foreshadow his relationship with Albertine. Though Proust deals only with the inhabitants of Sodom, his depiction and analysis of homosexual behaviour applies to Albertine and her friends as well as to Charlus and Morel.

Like other homosexual novelists, Proust had to devise a strategy that would allow him to portray inverts and include the drama of their lives in his fiction without sacrificing the interest and sympathy of his readers. Proust sets out to challenge the conventional assumptions about normal and perverse sexual behaviour and tries to prove, through the analogies and examples of a highly complex argument, that what is 'most ineptly termed homosexuality' is an infinitely varied aspect of human nature. He begins by presenting a concrete and rather shocking example of inversion that is witnessed by Marcel from a concealed vantage point. Marcel first discovers the true nature of the Baron by watching his seductive approach to Jupien and listening to their act of sodomy, for the violent and inarticulate sounds of masochistic pleasure, and the comparison to the murderer who must 'wash away the traces of a crime', leave little doubt as to what has occurred. Proust concentrates on producing the effect, not the substance, of the scene and omits any reference to

Marcel's reaction. By presenting the scene aurally rather than visually Proust subtly implicates the reader, who reconstructs the encounter in his imagination from the suggestive sounds.

After this scene, Proust distinguishes a great variety of homosexual types, and places this human species in the perspective of the natural order. This manoeuvre is daring, serious, sad, ironic and comic, and the tone of the entire Introduction, with its frequent shifts in logic and mood, is determined by the amoral and fatalistic attitude of Marcel. Though a great many of the characters in the novel are inverts, Proust deliberately places Marcel outside homosexual society, but allows him to retain an intimate knowledge and sympathetic understanding of its habits. Marcel's ambivalent mixture of compassion for the pain and suffering, and hostility to the 'vice' and folly of homosexuals is never resolved, for it reflects Proust's own narcissism and self-hatred.

Marcel, the enthusiastic voyeur and passive observer of inversion, takes his right to eavesdrop for granted, but explains in detail the reasons for his risky infiltration of the courtyard. He is curious and impatient to discover what is happening; he had been 'rewarded' for his previous daring by witnessing the revealing scene at Montjouvain; and he thinks of his courageous manoeuvre as a mock-heroic re-enactment of the escapades of the Boers and of the duels he had fought in defence of Dreyfus. Later on, he justifies his imprudent and morally dubious behaviour by explaining that his new-found knowledge of Charlus has finally enabled him to form a coherent picture of that complex character. All these reasons and justifications serve to emphasize rather than to disguise Marcel's fascination with inversion and delight in voyeurism, which in Proust's novel is much more than an expedient and rather unconvincing narrative device. Marcel's ostensibly detached and dispassionate point of view allows the narrator to evade the problem of his emotional involvement in and moral judgment of the scene he witnesses. But Marcel is actually a thinly disguised homosexual, compulsively pursuing opportunities to spy on the inverts who act out his own fantasies.

Marcel imagines himself as a moral botanist waiting to observe the pollination of a rare orchid by a bee; and the flower that awaits penetration in the courtyard of the Duchesse de Guermantes introduces the analogy between the sexual behaviour of men and plants which becomes increasingly complex. At first the botanical analogy has a grotesquely comic effect, for the shabby, posturing tailor is the orchid and the stout, middle-aged Baron the bee. Both men are coarse and unattractive, and their absurd ritualistic approach resembles an exotic mating dance and ends with the arrogant Charlus engaged in a coy post-coital dialogue.

But the analogy has an important function not only in relation to Charlus and Jupien but also to Proust's argument on the origins and prevalence of homosexuality in general. For he sees homosexuality as an intrinsic part of the manifold variety of species, of which Jupien is a 'sub-variety'. It is therefore a natural phenomenon, a fate as inescapable as the growth of a plant from a seed. Jupien is 'the man predestined to exist in order that [men like Charlus] may have their share of sensual pleasure on this earth; the man who cares only for elderly gentlemen' (i.9). The apparently unnatural conjunction of the Baron and Jupien is, paradoxically, quite natural for their species, and each is predestined to perform his sexual role. Their coupling is compared to a miracle 'almost of the same order and no less marvellous' than the fertilization of a rare orchid; and Marcel observes that 'As soon as I had considered their meeting from this point of view, everything about it seemed to me instinct with beauty' (i.39).

Proust considers the terms fertilize and sterility in several contexts, and compares the solitary homosexual with the sterile medusa that dies on the sand. Just as this jellyfish appears to be 'an exquisite wheel of azure flame' or 'the mauve orchid of the sea' if seen with the eyes of the natural historian or the aesthete, so Marcel's vision of Charlus and Jupien reveals that the invert can also be admired as a natural being with his own particular beauty. Since men, like plants, have sexuality, it is not surprising that there are as many ways of fulfilling it as there are of floral fertilization. Proust then extends the analogy to plead for acceptance of tastes even as rarefied as the Baron's:

M. de Charlus (and here the word fertilise must be understood in a moral sense, since in the physical sense the union of male with male is and must be sterile, but it is no small matter that a person may encounter the sole pleasure which he is capable of enjoying, and that every 'creature here below' can impart to some other 'his music, or his fragrance or his flame'), M. de Charlus was one of those men who may be called exceptional, because however many they may be, the satisfaction, so easy in others, of their sexual requirements depends upon the coincidence of too many conditions, and of conditions too difficult to ensure. (i.38)

Proust's determinism and quasi-'scientific' attitude express his acceptance of a condition that cannot be changed and a sympathy for Charlus and other inverts whose sexual difficulties are virtually insurmountable. The statement that Charlus and Jupien's act is 'beautiful' is both an ironic parody of botanical enthusiasm and a possibility that is seriously entertained. Proust, like his bisexual characters, tries to have it both ways.

From the example of Charlus and Jupien, and the statement that they cannot change their nature and are no more abnormal than any other sexual beings, Proust develops a detailed account of the kinds of homosexuals and varieties of suffering, and describes a witty and ironic gallery of homosexual characters. There is the propagandist; the transvestite; the beautiful young man who keeps a mistress but cannot help revealing his true nature by running after boxers; the jealousy and insecurity of the man who has a bisexual lover; and the solitary man who cannot bear the hypocrisy of his position and is destined to lonely sterility. Proust compares the survival of homosexuality to the survival of a faith, and emphasizes the freemasonry of inversion which extends to all levels of society and is the great democratizer of prodigious personages and microscopic animalcules.

Proust also gives an eloquent and tragic account of the inevitable life of deception and guilt, for homosexuals are a

Race upon which a curse weighs and which must live amid falsehood and perjury, because it knows the world to regard as a punishable and a scandalous, as an inadmissable thing, its desire, that which constitutes for every human creature the greatest happiness in life. (i.20)

They are also debarred from Christianity, from a true filial relationship, and from true and open friendship, since their motives are always thought questionable. Proust cites the example of Wilde, 'who one day was feasted at every table, applauded in every theatre in London, and on the next was driven from every lodging, unable to find a pillow on which to lay his head',[6] to show the precarious social position of the invert (i.22). Proust (who belonged to both 'races') then makes an elaborate comparison of homosexuals and Jews to explain how their ostracism and persecution affect their behaviour as a group. Like the Jews, who are eager to join a society that rejects them, homosexuals fawn on those of the 'other race' and despise their own kind.

Proust suggests that the perilous yet exciting intimacy of inverts makes their honour precarious and their liberty provisional, and excludes them not only from the sympathy of society but also of their fellows, in whom they inspire disgust and revulsion. They are condemned to a life of misery, 'shunning one another, seeking out those who are most directly their opposite, who do not desire their company' (i.22). Though their vice survives obdurate to every warning and punishment, it is considered more repugnant than other more comprehensible vices, and must remain clandestine and masked in deception: 'all of them [are] obliged to protect their own secret, but have their part in a secret shared with the others, which the rest of humanity does not suspect' (i.24).

Proust deals with two kinds of deception: the life of social lying, of public deceit, of those who play the game of duplicity that is bound to end in scandal and ruin; and the other more private deception, the cultivation of illusion that is necessary to achieve sexual satisfaction. For these men are

> lovers from whom is always precluded the possibility of that love the hope of which gives them the strength to endure so many risks and so much loneliness, since they fall in love with precisely that type of man who has nothing feminine about him, who is not an invert and consequently cannot love them in return; with the result that their desire would be forever insatiable did not their money procure for them real men, and their imagination end by making them take for real men the inverts to whom they had prostituted themselves. (i.21)

Homosexuals who are attracted by their opposites can buy the virile men they desire, but they will inevitably be forced to deceive themselves and create imaginatively a more acceptable reality in order to secure sexual satisfaction. This perceptive and paradoxical juxtaposition of hope and loneliness, imagination and prostitution, suggests their need to maintain illusions about the squalid reality of male love.

Proust believes that these covert aspects of homosexuality lend to it the mystique of an occult art whose intimates, like certain nocturnal animals, scent and attract one another from afar: 'The scattered Gomorrah tends, in every town, in every village, to reunite its separated members, to reform the biblical city while everywhere the same efforts are being made, be it in view of but a momentary reconstruction, by the nostalgic, the hypocritical, sometimes by the courageous exiles from Sodom' (i.349-50). These *cognoscenti* form a kind of sexual freemasonry, a strange and monstrous fraternity, part of society yet distinct from it, torn between desire, temptation and fear, and sworn to silence about their guilty secret.

The concluding note of the chapter unites Proust's 'scientific' analysis with his passages of social criticism. He warns that segregation of Sodomites in a new Sodom would be no solution to their sufferings because inverts doom themselves to a furtive existence. Though they often hate and fear heterosexual society, they ultimately believe in its values and desperately want to be a part of it.

II

The theme of painful and illusory love, represented by the paradigm of Swann and Odette, helps to structure and unite the multifarious strands of the lengthy and complex *Remembrance of Things Past*. This paradigm is repeated not only in the relations of Marcel and Albertine (which echo the earlier love of Marcel and Gilberte Swann) but also in those of Charlus and Morel. Marcel's knowledge of Swann's love for Odette affected him with the predestined pain of an insidious toxin, and he relates that it 'helped my imagination, in after years, to take the line of supposing that Albertine might, instead of being a good girl, have had the same immorality, the same faculty of deception as a reformed prostitute, and I thought of all the sufferings that would in that case have been in store for me had I ever really been her lover' (i.285).

Charlus, who tells Morel that Odette forced him to help her betray Swann with five or six other men, is himself betrayed by his lover, Morel. Though Morel is a homosexual, he is engaged to

Jupien's niece and carries on a private correspondence with the Racinean actress Léa, who is notorious for her exclusive interest in women and whose friendship with Albertine arouses the jealousy of Marcel. And Marcel's false confidence about Albertine's loyalty and surprising discovery that she has suddenly left him are portrayed in the illuminating perspective of Morel's betrayal of Charlus.

The primal scene of *Remembrance of Things Past*, in the sexual as well as the structural sense, takes place during the Combray idyll at Montjouvain, the house of the great but unrecognized composer Vinteuil. Mlle Vinteuil is always accompanied by a girl who is older than herself, has an evil reputation in the neighbourhood and finally moves permanently into Montjouvain. The old composer's heart is broken by his discovery of the sexual perversions of his beloved daughter, and she virtually kills her father who dies for her just as he had lived for her.

The young Marcel has his first and most important voyeuristic experience at Montjouvain. He sees Mlle Vinteuil and her lesbian lover exciting each other sexually as the friend vilifies her dead father and spits on his photograph, which bears a distinct likeness to his daughter. The psychological connection between the ritualistic profanation of a parent's sacred memory and the perverse pleasures of homosexuality reverberates throughout the novel. It introduces the innocent Marcel to sadism and that indifference to the suffering of others which 'is the one true, terrible and lasting form of cruelty',[7] and reveals that a diabolic identification with evil and the posthumous denial of a parent's love intensify sexual excitement.

Marcel's jealous suspicions about Albertine are first aroused when Doctor Cottard, drawing no doubt on his vast physiological knowledge, observes her dancing with her friend Andrée and informs Marcel: 'They are certainly keenly roused. It is not sufficiently known that women derive most excitement from their breasts. And theirs' as you see, are completely touching' (i.273). Marcel would never have suspected Albertine of being in love with Andrée if Cottard had not drawn attention to their contiguity; and when he confronts her with the accusation she disingenuously denies it with 'a peremptory word unsupported by proof': ' "If it had been true, I should have told you. But Andrée and I both loathe that sort of thing. We have not lived all these years without seeing women with cropped hair who behave like men and do the things you mean, and nothing revolts us more"' (i.324). Though Marcel does not know it, this denial expresses the characteristic hatred and deliberate rivalry of covert for overt homosexuals, whom they see as a caricature of their own behaviour, a mirror that accentuates every blemish they refuse to recognize in themselves.

It is highly ironic that Saint-Loup's advances to Albertine dispel Marcel's suspicions about her relations with women, for his chivalric attentions (like his marriage to Gilberte and affair with Rachel) are made only to disguise his homosexuality. In this respect Saint-Loup repeats the manoeuvre of his uncle Charlus, whose advances to Odette, tolerated by the knowing Swann, excited rumours that camouflaged the Baron's taste for men.

In the final chapter of *Cities of the Plain* Marcel tells his mother that he has irrevocably decided not to marry Albertine and that he plans to stop seeing her. But at their next meeting Albertine, without realizing the incriminating implications of her remark, tells Marcel that she spent several years in Trieste with the friend of Mlle Vinteuil and that she knows the composer's daughter as well as she had known her friend. Albertine's casual and alarming revelation sharpens Marcel's obscure doubts into a clear focus and immediately revives the noxious image of the desecration scene at Montjouvain. It is significant that Marcel, who is shocked to find himself implicated in 'the fatal consequences which evil actions indefinitely engender' (i.362), sees Albertine's connection with 'a practising and professional Sapphist' and the undreamed of sufferings that open before him as a retribution for having 'allowed' his grandmother to die. Marcel feels he has been punished for not loving his grandmother — and his mother — enough, although his passionate feeling for them has prevented him from loving Albertine.

Marcel then asks himself, 'with a girl as pretty as Albertine, was it possible that Mlle Vinteuil, having the desires she had, had not asked her to gratify them?' And he inevitably answers, 'the proof that Albertine had not been shocked by the [sexual] request but had consented, was that they had not quarrelled, indeed their intimacy had steadily increased' (ii.365). By the same perverse logic, the knowledge of Albertine's lesbianism makes her more interesting, more desirable and more important to Marcel, and leads to a greater intimacy rather than to a rupture. The jealous Marcel now wants to have the woman who seems impossible to possess, and who challenges his power to attract and redeem her. Since Albertine has — in Marcel's mind — become directly involved with Mlle Vinteuil's profanation of her parent, the sexual excitement of that primal experience is now associated with and available through her.

After Albertine's disclosure, Marcel invites her to live in his Paris flat and guards her like a prisoner. He thus masochistically prolongs his torture of suspicion and fear, and combines his guilty sexual life with a loving devotion to his mother. This situation corresponds to Proust's description of how the woman who is 'imprisoned' within the body of a homosexual, contrives 'so ingeniously by herself, without instruction from anyone, to make use of the narrowest apertures in her prison wall to find what was necessary to her existence'. Even if the homosexual has a mistress who (like Marcel) chastises him and 'locks him up', the unconscious but visible woman in him will instinctively and inevitably 'seek the masculine organ' (i.29-30). When Albertine finally escapes from his vigilance in *The Sweet Cheat Gone*, Andrée's revelation that while living with him Albertine had betrayed him with Morel, with girls who had been corrupted and supplied by Morel, and with Andrée herself, once again emphasizes Proust's portrayal of the instability, anguish and treachery of homosexual love.

The description of Marcel and Albertine's affair adds another dimension of Proustian dissimulation, for he portrays his own homosexual love in a heterosexual disguise. Albertine's liaison with the passive Marcel and her lesbian infidelities are really transpositions of male love convincingly projected on to a woman.[8] Their relationship is based on the kind of mutual deception and mutual disillusionment that is analysed in the Introduction, for Albertine is actually attracted to Marcel's feminine qualities just as he is to her masculine ones. Marcel is one of those transparent homosexuals who 'seek out those women who love other women' and 'enjoy with such women the same pleasure as with a man . . . For, in the relations which they have with her, they play, for the woman who loves her own sex, the part of another woman, and she offers them at the same time more or less what they find in other men' (i.31-2).

The homosexual core of *Cities of the Plain* concerns the relationship of the handsome and talented violinist, Charles Morel, and the satanically brilliant Baron de Charlus, the younger brother of the

Duc de Guermantes. Proust portrays Charlus with both love and hate, and he is the most complex and profound character in the novel. Charlus is an extremely intelligent aristocrat who is proud of his distinguished lineage and traditions, and (as his grave illness later reveals) a pious and even fervent Christian. He has 'rare moral qualities', is sympathetic and generous, capable of affection and devotion, but hides his amenity and kindness behind a mask of false brutality. As Proust ironically observes, when the Baron transforms his mansion into a military hospital during the war, he yields 'less to his passion than to his good heart'. But the obsession that dominates his life, betrays his intellect, brings out the worst side of his nature and dooms him to unhappiness is his passion for young men.

Though Charlus prides himself on his own virility, considers other men odiously effeminate and is attracted by Morel's 'girlish air enshrined in masculine beauty', he belongs 'to that race of beings, less paradoxical than they appear, whose ideal is manly simply because their temperament is feminine and who in their life resemble in appearance only the rest of men' (i.20). Though shrewd and suspicious, Charlus lacks self-awareness, and when he flaunts his perversity to intensify his pleasure, he fails to notice how repellent he appears. At the height of his affair with Morel, Marcel observes him waddling through a crowded salon like a *grande dame* hampered by an imaginary skirt, 'balancing a pursy stomach and an almost symbolical behind' as the cruel light of day exposes his dyed moustaches, lipstick and rouge. Charlus maintains his artificial vitality by sheer force of will, and when he is humiliated by Morel his façade cracks and the tears trickle down and melt the paint beneath his eyes.

The homosexual relationships in Proust's novel represent a struggle for power that transcends the barriers of snobbism and social class, and that is also reflected in the opposition of aristocracy and bourgeoisie, Jews and Christians, Dreyfusards and anti-Dreyfusards. Though Albertine has a dubious past and is financially dependent upon Marcel as Odette was upon Swann, Rachel upon Saint-Loup, and Morel upon Charlus, the sexual power inevitably remains with the lower-class lover who is contemptuous of those he attracts, and whose ingratitude and infidelity subject his supposed master to rage and anguish. As Proust observes in the final volume: 'Morel was [Charlus'] master if he did not yield to him . . . The disgust of distinguished people for snobs who want to force themselves upon them, the virile man has for the invert, the woman for every man who is too much in love with her.'⁹

Morel, who lacks the redeeming qualities of the Baron and is perhaps the most vile and unattractive character in the novel, is sexually involved with Albertine as well as with the Prince de Guermantes, Charlus and Saint-Loup. He responds to the Baron's attentions in order to exploit his wealth and social position, and to advance his own career as a musician. It is therefore doubly ironic that Charlus is introduced into the circle of the bourgeois social climbers, the Verdurins, as a friend of Morel (whose father was the valet of Marcel's Uncle Adolphe — the lover of Odette, the lady in pink), just as Swann had previously joined it as a friend of Odette. Moreover, since the aristocracy is always more tolerant of sexual irregularities than the middle class, nobody in the Faubourg Saint-Germain ever refers to Charlus' morals, though they are 'denounced daily far from the circle in which he moved, just as, at times, the sound of artillery fire is audible only beyond a zone of silence' (ii.67).

Morel is unaware that Charlus' *entrée* into the Verdurins' band of faithful followers indicates the diminution of his social power, and the Baron strives to maintain his former dignity and status in this inferior milieu by openly expressing his scorn in a dry and cutting tone of voice. When, for example, Madame Verdurin begins to grow familiar, tries to equalize their social status with a clumsy jest and asks Charlus if he knows 'of any ruined old nobleman in your Faubourg who would come to me as a porter', Charlus (who cannot foresee that his cousin, the ruined Prince de Guermantes, will one day come to her as a husband) sardonically replies: 'I don't advise it... I should be afraid for your sake, that your smart visitors would call at the lodge and go no farther' (ii.157).

The relationship between the well-born Charlus and the proletarian Morel (who begs Marcel not to disclose his antecedents) is based on their common interest in sex and art, and is parodied in a Chaucerian *conte* about the devious stratagems and indelicate deceptions of love. In one of the most brilliantly comic scenes in the novel, the Prince de Guermantes picks up Morel and arranges a meeting at a brothel. Charlus, who discovers what has happened without learning that the Prince is the seducer, hires Jupien to arrange a hiding place so that he can spy on Morel. The Baron is extremely nervous among the unfamiliar whores and outraged by the delays which allow Morel to discover he has been trapped by the Baron and to escape from the Prince. When a new place of assignation is confirmed, Morel arrives to find that the Prince has indiscreetly decorated the room with his family photographs (an echo of Mlle Vinteuil and of Proust himself) which include one of the Baron. Morel again flees, the Prince is again bewildered and frustrated, and 'Charlus was protected from a betrayal which filled him with despair, and avenged, without ever having imagined such a thing, still less how it came about' (ii.315). This incident emphasizes the objective absurdity of these sexual machinations and the subjective confusion of the characters who are trapped by their emotions.

It is clear that Charlus derives sado-masochistic pleasure from his liaison with Morel. Even his ironic reference to the musician as 'a good little boy, obedient, and well-behaved' gives him some sadistic delight from the use of the chaste comparison, which emphasizes the contrast between Morel's supposed character and the actual pain he inflicts on the Baron. Charlus also derives sadistic satisfaction when he learns that Morel has 'outraged' his fiancée, Jupien's niece, and then dropped her without compunction, for as Morel's jealous lover the Baron enjoys her pain at the same time that he imagines himself suffering in her place.

The sado-masochistic *dénouement* of the Charlus-Morel affair takes place in *The Captive* after Morel has given a dazzling performance of Vinteuil's music before a distinguished gathering from the Faubourg. The guests, who have been invited to the Verdurins by the Baron, pay their snobbish respects to him and ignore the hostess. When the Verdurins find they can no longer endure the arrogance and rudeness of the Baron they revenge themselves by telling Morel about Charlus' duplicity and evil reputation, his sexual designs on the violinist and (what is most effective) the latter's humiliating position in the eyes of society. This malice provokes Morel's hysterical public denunciation of the entirely unsuspecting Charlus, who is rejoicing in the triumph of his *protegé*:

'Leave me alone, I forbid you to come near me,' Morel shouted at

> the Baron. 'You know what I mean all right, I'm not the first
> young man you've tried to corrupt!' . . .
> 　　One saw M. de Charlus dumb, stupefied, measuring the depths
> of his misery without understanding its cause, finding not a word
> to utter, raising his eyes to stare at each of the company in turn,
> with a questioning, outraged, suppliant air.[10]

Charlus is so surprised and shocked by these just though hypocritical
accusations that, for the first time in his life, he is absolutely
speechless; and he disappoints Marcel's hope that an explosion of
rage will demolish the violinist.

At this intensely humiliating (and therefore painfully pleasurable)
moment, when the lion-tamer is devoured, the powerful loyalties of
the aristocracy are reaffirmed. The Queen of Naples, who had an
unshakable attachment to her friends, her family and all the Princes
of her race, including Charlus, returns to the Verdurin salon to
recover her priceless fan, witnesses the degradation of the Baron,
and rescues him from his shattering disgrace 'with a marvellously
detached intonation, which wrung from M. de Charlus, despite his
broken heart, a smile of expert and delighted appreciation of the art
of impertinence'.[11] The Queen takes the Baron on her arm, refuses
Morel the honour of being presented to her and leaves the house with
a splendid sweep of her gown.

When Charlus reappears in the final volume, *Time Regained*, his
moral and physical degeneration have advanced to the 'extreme
point where the small primitive personality of the individual, his
ancestral qualities, were entirely obscured by the interposition of the
defect or generic evil which accompanied them' (*TR*, 80). Morel and
Charlus have inevitably become bitter enemies after their rupture:
the musician pursues the Baron with implacable hatred and the
Baron plans to murder him. Sadistic pleasure has become the
dominant pursuit of Charlus' life, 'sexual gratification was insepar-
able from the idea of cruelty and (how strong this was I did not then
realize) the man who attracted him seemed like a kind of delightful
executioner' (*TR*, 97).

In a fashion that has become quite familiar after Montjouvain and
the courtyard of the Duchess, Marcel secretly prowls around
Jupien's brothel until he discovers the unfortunate Charlus at the
height of masochistic mortification:

'I implore you, pity, pity, unloose me, unchain me, do not strike me so hard,' said a voice. 'I kiss your feet, I humiliate myself, I won't do it again, have pity' . . . And I heard the crack of a cat-o'-nine tails probably loaded with nails for it was followed by cries of pain . . . There on the bed, like Prometheus bound to his rock, squirming under the strokes of a cat-o'-nine tails, which was, as a matter of fact, loaded with nails, wielded by Maurice, already bleeding and covered with bruises, which proved he was not submitting to the torture for the first time, I saw before me M. de Charlus. (*TR*, 144)[12]

Whatever words are spoken in a context so far removed from normal experience are bound to seem false, and that is part of the intended effect, for the emotions at the actual moment of flagellation are so complex that no words can possibly express them. (The literary — and cinematic — tradition is for the man to clench his teeth and bear his involuntary punishment in silence.) The ironic reference to Prometheus, a classical Christ-figure, is emphasized by the unheroic 'squirming'; and the final revelation that Charlus is being beaten is disclosed from the superior vantage point of Marcel, who can participate in the voyeuristic experience without risking or exposing his own emotions.

Though Maurice looks enough like Morel to give Charlus the illusion of being whipped by him, his thirst for evil cannot be satisfied even by the cat-o'-nine tails; and the Baron complains to Jupien with extraordinary delicacy: 'I did not want to speak before that little fellow. He's very nice and does his best but he's not brutal enough' (*TR*, 147). Proust cannot resist, in this anticlimax, exposing the ridiculous aspect of Charlus' eagerness for punishment and degradation.

After such a taxing experience it is hardly surprising that the Baron has an apoplectic stroke at the end of the novel, lapses into a second childhood and appears, for the last time, as

A man with glazed eyes and bent body who was deposited rather than sitting in the back of [a car], and was making efforts to hold himself straight such as a child makes when told to behave nicely. An untouched forest of snow-white hair escaped from under his straw hat while a white beard like those snow attaches to statues in public gardens depended from his chin. It was M. de Charlus sitting beside Jupien (prodigal of attentions) convalescing from an attack of apoplexy. (*TR*, 200-1)

Even when he becomes blind Charlus refuses to abandon his homosexual pursuits and develops a taste for young boys. In contrast to Charlus, his nephew Robert de Saint-Loup has been a heroic and idealized figure. But in *The Sweet Cheat Gone* Marcel is astounded to discover from Jupien and then to see for himself that Morel is the lover of Saint-Loup. In *Time Regained* the suspicion that he has seen Saint-Loup leave Jupien's brothel after amusing himself in an equivocal fashion is confirmed when the excited Jupien finds a profaned *croix-de-guerre* on the floor of the house, and when Saint-Loup unexpectedly calls at Marcel's flat to look for the medal he has lost. Saint-Loup returns to the front without the medal and is killed in action the following day while gallantly protecting the retreat of his men. Marcel's maid Françoise, who becomes the moral touchstone in the novel after the death of his mother, is more profoundly affected by the death of Saint-Loup than she was by that of Albertine, who had lived in Marcel's flat and later died after a fall from a horse.[13] Proust, who thoroughly enjoyed his military service, tests his characters by their courage in war: Saint-Loup's sacrificial death allows him to recapture some of his lost glory, while the news that Morel has been arrested for desertion merely confirms his moral corruption.

Proust's extensive homosexual underground includes — besides Marcel — Mlle Vinteuil and her friend, Odette and her lesbian lovers, Léa and Andrée, Madame Cottard's nephew, Jupien, Aimé, Nissim Bernard, Morel, the Prince de Guermantes and Charlus. The unexpected addition of Albertine and Saint-Loup reveal a new and surprising aspect of their personalities, a 'reverse side of the fabric' which explains, while it complicates, their role in the novel. The sexual contamination and violent deaths of Marcel's fiancée and greatest friend also reveal Proust's need to implicate, condemn and punish his characters — and through them himself — for his profound sense of guilt about the betrayal of his mother's love. Proust is precisely like those homosexuals 'who succeed in concealing the fact that they belong to [the race] they readily unmask, with a view less to injuring them, though they have no scruple about that, than to *excusing themselves*' (i.23). In the bitter description of Jupien's brothel in *Time Regained*, Proust likens its fate to that of Sodom and Gomorrah, and of Pompeii, and imagines that the volcanic eruptions of the German bombardment of Paris are a prelude to the catastrophe that will reduce the house to ashes by the avenging fire of heaven. It is as difficult to find righteous men in Proust's world as in the Cities of the Plain.

Proust's characters are all seen subjectively and relatively, and he writes that 'however multiform may be the person with whom we are in love, she can in any case offer us two essential personalities accordingly as she appears to us as ours, or as turning her desires in another direction' (i.325). With the exception of Jupien and Charlus all the characters are capable of deception and infidelity with lovers of both sexes, and they move in a shifting world of distressing uncertainties and fresh betrayals. For Proust there is no absolute but art, which represents an unchanging reality and contemplative calm that is a soothing contrast to the passion and flux of human relationships.

The prominent homosexual theme in Proust's novel is closely related to his attitude toward his mother and his inversion as well as to the discovery of his true purpose in life: his artistic vocation. As an invalid whose asthmatic attacks led to moments of intense pain and exhaustion; as a Jew and Dreyfusard pardoning rebuffs and flattered by condescension; as a homosexual doomed to constant duplicity and obliged to make a secret of his life; and as a writer whose great work, by its very existence, profaned his mother while it triumphantly vindicated his dedication to art, Proust, with all his worldliness and charm, stood clearly outside the society he portrayed and anatomized with such subtlety and perception. Proust's compulsive fascination with voyeurism connected — through the associations of involuntary memory — the masochistic pleasures of profanation and inversion. This insight led Proust to reject the illusion of love for the permanence of art.

VI

CONRAD

Victory

Critics of *Victory* (1915) invariably quote what is taken to be the
theme of the novel — 'woe to the man whose heart has not learned
while young to hope, to love — and to put its trust in life!'[1] — and
many of them use this concluding passage to exemplify the supposed
weaknesses of the book: the obvious theme, wooden characters and
melodramatic plot.[2] Guerard writes: 'The novel remains ambivalent
or perhaps only uncertain concerning a tenderness to be distinguished from love; and does not do much with the faint suggestion
that the psychic and spiritual failure is also sexual'.[3]

But Lena's emotional responsiveness, capacity to love and trust in
life are negated by Heyst's sexual failure. And the idea that a
woman's sacrificial devotion can redeem a man who is incapable of
love is undermined by a concurrent and even more powerful theme:
that homosexuals, who represent a withdrawal from normal human
relations and a denial of life, are doomed and damned beyond
redemption. A careful analysis of Conrad's discreet but quite
intentional sexual allusions reveals the subtle tension between the
overt and covert themes, and the *complex* motivation of the
characters. It also suggests that the extravagant emotions and violent
actions are inspired by the perverse sexual passions that surge
beneath the surface of the novel.

Conrad's portrayal of the misogynist Jones, an evil homosexual
who nevertheless has the most impressive speeches in the novel,
reveals that he was fascinated and frightened by sexual perversion.[4]
But the literary and social conventions of the time (which made
characters like Ricardo call his enemies 'ill-conditioned skunks' and
'animated cucumbers') precluded any direct discussion of this
theme. When Macdonald Hastings, who was dramatizing the novel,
asked Conrad to explain the character of Jones, he evasively replied:

'There is a strain of peculiar craziness about the gentleman. The novel only faintly suggests it.'[5] It is therefore not true, as Moser suggests, that Conrad is confused and 'simply does not know what he wants to make of Heyst',[6] for *Victory* is a deliberate compromise between Conrad's desire to write openly about homosexuality and his need to suppress the theme and to surround the sexual core of the novel with reticence and evasion. This conventional restriction exaggerated Conrad's characteristic tendency toward ambiguity, allusiveness and abstraction, for as he wrote to Richard Curle:

> Explicitness, my dear fellow, is fatal to the glamour of all artistic work, robbing it of all suggestiveness, destroying all illusion . . . Nothing is more clear than the utter insignificance of explicit statement, and also its power to call the attention away from things that matter in the region of art.[7]

Conrad's extremely complex narration, in which the action shifts back and forth in time and is usually related indirectly, makes it impossible to know exactly what is going on between Morrison and Heyst, Heyst and Lena, Lena and Ricardo, or Ricardo and Jones: the sexual relationships of all the characters remain ambiguous. Their story is related partly by a representative white man in Java and partly by Captain Davidson, who could not possibly be aware of the dialogue of Heyst and Lena when they are alone on Samburan. Davidson, like Captain Mitchell in *Nostromo*, is a kindly, *normal* figure who is incapable of understanding the strange sexuality of Jones and Ricardo and dismisses them as grotesque rascals. His lack of insight ironically underlines the contrast between the conventional and the subterranean themes.

Conrad also accentuates the ambiguity of the characters by emphasizing their extreme isolation and the unreality of the exotic setting. And all the characters deceive each other, for base or noble motives. Heyst, Lena and Mrs Schomberg deceive Schomberg, Schomberg deceives Jones and Ricardo, Ricardo twice deceives Jones, Lena deceives Ricardo, Wang deceives Heyst, and both Heyst and Lena fear they have been deceived by each other. At the violent climax of the novel Heyst, Lena, Jones and Ricardo meet their death in a chaos of misapprehension. Finally, even the minor characters are not what they seem to be. Zangiacomo is really a German with a dyed beard; the oppressed and terrified Mrs Schomberg hides behind a mask and is quite capable of resolute action; the manly military, bearded and broad-chested Schomberg is actually a coward; and 'plain Mr Jones' is neither plain, nor a gentleman, nor Jones.

Victory is structured by a recurrent pattern of human relationships. Heyst's rescue of Lena is like his rescue of Morrison, Ricardo's assault on Lena is like Schomberg's, Lena's dependence on Heyst is like Ricardo's dependence on Jones, and Ricardo's tenuous control of the violent Pedro is like Jones' control of Ricardo. Even Wang's relation to his wife, whom he persuades to run away with him and then keeps safely hidden in the jungle, parodies Heyst's inability to protect Lena. The effect of this intricate pattern is to bind all the characters in a common tragic destiny and to emphasize the irony of Heyst's desire to remain detached and isolated — invulnerable because elusive.

Heyst's relationship with Morrison is introduced as a subject of speculation and gossip: 'Heyst became associated with Morrison on terms about which people were in doubt.' No one knew the real reason why they became partners because each wanted to keep it hidden: Morrison out of embarrassment, Heyst out of delicacy. A rumour soon sprang up that Heyst, 'having obtained some mysterious hold on Morrison, had fastened himself on him and was sucking him dry', and Schomberg warned people not to get caught in Heyst's web. But the narrator makes it clear that when Heyst rescued Morrison from the Portuguese authorities on Timor, he soothed him and shared his distress. Unlike the traders who had a wife in every port, Morrison was 'rather ascetic than otherwise'. He begged Heyst, like a lover, not to 'spurn and ruin him', and urged Heyst to become a partner and retrieve his money, though Morrison's foolish generosity had ruined his trading ventures. So Heyst, the temperamental opposite of Morrison, became the victim of Morrison's emotional demands.

Morrison's pathetic belief that Heyst was his divine saviour, and Heyst's feeling that he had rescued Morrison from one fate only to deliver him to a worse one, made Heyst 'deem himself guilty of Morrison's death'. Thus Schomberg's venomous slanders that their homosexual friendship suddenly ended when Heyst discarded Morrison and sent him to die in England, which Lena repeats to Heyst, exacerbate his sensitivity and guilt, and makes him more vulnerable to the evil designs of Jones.

When Heyst first tells Lena about Morrison he is unaware that she
has already heard Schomberg's version of the story. He mentions
'some hidden weakness' in his character and emphasizes the
similarity of his relationship to Morrison and to Lena: 'I use the word
[cornered] because it expresses the man's situation exactly, and
because you just used it yourself.' Lena's response to this casual
allusion is extremely emotional:

> 'What do you say?' she whispered, astounded. 'A man!'
> Heyst laughed at her wondering eyes.
> 'No! No! I mean in his own way.'
> 'I knew very well that it couldn't be anything like that,' she
> observed under her breath. (168)

Heyst's forced laughter disguises his uneasiness about Lena's violent
reaction. His reassurance that Morrison was cornered by financial
trouble is met by her *sotto voce* relief that Morrison was not, as she
had feared, a cornered homosexual.

When Heyst actually mentions the name of Morrison Lena repeats
it in an appalled tone, suddenly realizes that her rescuer was involved
with Morrison and is profoundly upset. She then astounds him by
repeating Schomberg's accusation that 'there never were two such
loving friends to look at as you two; then, when you got all you
wanted out of him and got thoroughly tired of him, too, you kicked
him out to go home and die' (180). And this, of course, is what the
insecure Lena fears will happen if Heyst also grows weary of her
clinging emotional demands and awkward attempts to express her
gratitude. Despite Heyst's strenuous denials, there is something
about his character and behaviour that makes Lena retain her
suspicions about his dubious relations with Morrison. Her doubts
about his rectitude have the moral effect of a stab in the back and help
to undermine his resistance to Jones and Ricardo.

Lena is the focus of passion in the novel and inspires powerful
emotions in Schomberg, Heyst and Ricardo, though none of them is
sexually successful with her. Both Schomberg and Heyst offer to
liberate Lena from Zangiacomo's musical bondage and to provide
her with protection and security. The difference between them, of
course, is that the ludicrous Schomberg, the victim of a belated
passion, revolts Lena with his crude sexual demands while the more
passive and gentlemanly Heyst (who shrinks from the idea of

competition with Schomberg) merely says, 'Pray command me'. Lena runs away with Heyst not because she is attracted to his bald head and long moustaches but because she is desperate to escape from both Zangiacomo and Schomberg. And Mrs Schomberg, who knows that her husband wants to get rid of her, helps Lena not out of sympathy and charity but out of a desire to protect her own marriage and security.

Though Schomberg disliked Heyst before the arrival of Lena (because of his involvement with Morrison and his aloofness and even his temperate drinking habits), the thwarted passion, the wounded vanity and especially the humiliation of being deceived and defeated by someone he considered far less virile than himself are responsible for his violent hatred. Schomberg also feels that, like Heyst, Jones and Ricardo use his hotel as a base for their secret plots against him. And when he concocts the story of Heyst's treasure and sends the avenging furies to Samburan, he hopes to free himself from their dangerous presence at the same time that he destroys Heyst and Lena. Ricardo represents Schomberg's lust for Lena just as Jones manifests his hatred of Heyst.[8]

Heyst's ambivalent rescue of Lena, which is prompted by a generous feeling that his father would have defined as a form of contempt called pity, is both a repetition of his sympathetic response to Morrison and an unusually impulsive act. Heyst is known as a 'queer chap', completely detached from 'feminine associations' and even earthly passions. And when Davidson hears that his friend has run off with Lena he can hardly believe it and exclaims: 'He's not the man for it . . . being a gentleman only makes it worse.' Davidson's statement is ambiguous, but like Schomberg, Ricardo and Jones, he seems to question Heyst's manliness. By calling Heyst a gentleman he not only stresses the social differences between Heyst and Lena, but also uses the term that is constantly applied to Jones and that Jones derisively applies to Heyst in order to link the Swede with himself. When Heyst first looks at Lena (whose face is not described) he had 'the sensation of a new experience'. They immediately reverse their male and female roles as Lena challenges him to do something to save her and Heyst, hiding his ineffectuality behind a cavalier statement, says 'What would you wish me to do?'

Heyst and Lena have nothing to say to each other, either in Sourabaya or Samburan, and their basic lack of communication is symbolized by the profound silence of the island. Heyst's emotions are severely repressed and Lena cannot eliminate the fear and distrust of women that he inherited from his father. Heyst defensively insists that he is sceptical and has no illusions, and even when his heart becomes 'infected' he never forgets how easily women betray men.

Like Lena, Heyst never knew his mother and was devoted to his father, a kind of third-rate Schopenhauer whose books were ignored by the world and whose only disciple was his unfortunate son, who failed to learn *while young* to put his trust in life.[9] His father's portrait and library dominate Heyst's small house on Samburan and emphasize his permanent influence, and Lena's tenderness, love and self-sacrifice cannot overcome Heyst's spiritual and emotional starvation. Kierkegaard's perceptive analysis of his own father's destructive love helps to elucidate Heyst's relation to his father as well as to Lena:

> Once upon a time there lived a father and a son. Both were very gifted, both witty, particularly the father . . . On one rare occasion, when the father looking upon his son saw he was deeply troubled, he stood before him and said: poor child, you go about in silent despair. (But he never questioned him more closely, alas he could not, for he himself was in silent despair.) Otherwise, they never exchanged a word on the subject. Both father and son were, perhaps, two of the most melancholy men in the memory of man.
>
> And the father believed that he was the cause of the son's melancholy, and the son believed that he was the cause of the father's melancholy, and so they never discussed it . . . And what is the meaning of this? The point precisely is that he made me unhappy — but out of love. His error did not consist in lack of love but in mistaking a child for an old man.[10]

The passive Nordic gloom of both the Kierkegaards and the Heysts is characterized by a melancholy atmosphere, mutual unhappiness, lack of understanding, failure to communicate and silent despair.

Lena tells Heyst that she will stand by him as she once stood by her father; and after she has helped Ricardo to escape from her room, Heyst (who has failed to protect her against Ricardo) assumes his fatherly role and puts the exhausted Amazon to bed as if she were a child. Though Heyst feels more comfortable in the role of a father than of a lover, Lena refuses to be filial, transposes her repressed feelings from Ricardo to Heyst and experiences a kind of vicarious orgasm:

> She felt the woman's need to give way, the sweetness of surrender . . . She was surprised by a wave of languid weakness that came over her, embracing and enveloping her like warm water, with a noise in her ears as of a breaking sea. (251)

Lena quite naturally complained of her solitude in Schomberg's hotel, and seemed white and spectral when Heyst first embraced her. But on the island, when she falls in love with Heyst, Lena is still intensely lonely and feels that her very existence depends on a man who is unable to respond to her love and to satisfy her desperate need for emotional reassurance. Lena's fears are intensified by Wang, who seems to vanish out of existence rather than out of sight; and she tells Heyst: 'if you were to stop thinking of me I shouldn't be in the world at all . . . I can only be what you think I am.'

Lena's ontological fears and sense of unreality are presumably caused by her lack of sexual relations with Heyst, who has never slept with her and is unable to do so. They are in the archetypal romantic situation of lovers alone (for three months) on a desert island, and though Heyst's vanity is flattered by the (nominal) possession of a woman and Lena's by a belief that she can provide the absolute sacrifice that will satisfy Heyst's obscure needs, they are both deluded and unhappy. Heyst attempts to defend his emotional sterility and sexual impotence by alluding to his 'hidden weakness', suggesting that love *prevents* sex and stating that 'when one's heart has been broken into the way you have broken into mine, all sorts of weaknesses are free to enter'. Heyst's complaint makes Lena feel guilty about *his* sexual inadequacies as well as her sexual desires. She rather fearfully asks 'What more do you want from me?'; he seems to want companionship without emotional responsibility and answers, 'The impossible, I suppose'. And her pathetic apology: 'I only wish I could give you something more, or better, or whatever it is you want' (177), suggests she is both frightened and desperate.

Their mutual misunderstanding is so complete that when Heyst hides Lena from Jones and Ricardo for her safety, she thinks he is ashamed of her. Lena's almost suicidal desire for self-sacrifice is at once an attempt to punish herself for living 'unlawfully' with Heyst, to compensate for Heyst's impotence by elevating their relationship to a higher plane, and to make herself worthy of his love. The abject Lena realizes that she can never hope to understand or to satisfy Heyst, and feels ashamed of her emotions, 'as if her passion were of a hopelessly lower quality, unable to appease some exalted and delicate desire of his superior soul' (268). This is Lena's rationalization of the superiority of Heyst's coldness to her all-too-human passion.

Heyst's sexual doubts and fears are intensified by Lena's guilty confession: 'I am not what they call a good girl.' This allusion to her previous sexual experience — the inevitable result of an abandoned childhood and the hopeless grip of poverty — confirms Schomberg's accusation (euphemistically expressed in the novel) that Lena is a whore: 'He shot out an infamous word which made Davidson start. That's what the girl was.' Lena's admission also lends substance to Ricardo's claim (which parallels Jones' claim about Heyst) that he and Lena have a great deal in common. Most important, it worries and intimidates Heyst (though not, as Lena thinks, for moral reasons) by forcing him to compare his own lack of 'feminine associations' with Lena's extensive experience.

Heyst reveals that he has neither conscious nor subconscious desires for women and tells her directly: 'I've never killed a man nor loved a woman — not even in my thoughts, not even in my dreams ... To slay, to love — the greatest enterprises of life upon a man! And I have no experience of either' (178). Just after this assertion Heyst and Lena have an apparently unsatisfactory sexual encounter. 'With her hand she signed imperiously to him to leave her alone — a command which Heyst did not obey' (181). The next chapter begins, according to novelistic convention, as they get up from the ground and Lena arranges her hair while Heyst retrieves her sun helmet. It is significant that Heyst makes his unusual overture at the very moment he 'detests' Lena for believing Schomberg's slanders and is 'disgusted' with himself for being contaminated by the evil in the world. His approach to her is inspired not by love or passion, but by a resolute desire to overcome his feelings of inadequacy and to experience one of the two 'greatest enterprises of life'.

It is clear from their subsequent dialogue that Heyst's inept sexual advances have failed to satisfy Lena and merely heightened her belief that he does not love her. They also intensify Heyst's feeling of incompleteness and of 'the *physical* and moral sense of the *imperfections* of their relations' (186). When they return home he goes straight to his books and tries to sanction (or rationalize) his dissatisfaction with one of his father's philosophical epigrams: 'Of the stratagems of life the most cruel is the consolation of love — the most subtle, too; for the desire is the bed of dreams' (184). Lena seems to challenge this high-minded cynicism with the frank accusation: 'You should try to love me!' Heyst replies in confusion, 'Try . . . but it seems to me —', and then falls silent. Though his sexual attempt has been unsuccessful, he comforts himself with his favourite belief that 'he who forms a tie is lost. The germ of corruption has entered into his soul'.[11]

The difference between Lena's and Heyst's view of reality is reflected in her desire for a victorious self-sacrifice and his belief that she has corrupted their Eden. As Lena recklessly plans to disarm Ricardo and save Heyst, even at the cost of her own life, Heyst (especially at the moment he watches Ricardo kissing Lena's feet) sees Lena as the disobedient Eve who awakens the original Adam in him and introduces evil into their paradise.[12] He quite unjustly blames her for the intrusion of Jones and Ricardo and for the treachery and desertion of Wang.

Heyst realizes that his inability to love is related to his inability to kill, but he is unable to assert himself when Jones and Ricardo invade the island and Wang steals his revolver. While Ricardo strokes his knife and Jones fondles his gun, Heyst is profoundly aware that he is disarmed, without a weapon, 'not sufficiently equipped', that is, unmanned and impotent in the physical as well as the sexual sense. Whereas Schomberg felt that he lost his courage when he lost Lena and would be a much stronger man if she were at his side ('a pair of woman's arms, flung round his neck, would brace him up for the encounter. Inspire him'), Heyst feels that Lena weakens him, makes him vulnerable, and forces him to lie, to cringe and to humiliate himself for her sake: 'All his defences were broken now. Life had him fairly by the throat.' By contrast, Lena is inspired by Heyst's affection and seems to grow in physical as well as moral stature. In Schomberg's hotel she seemed small, weak and frightened, but when Ricardo first spies her 'she loomed up strangely big and shadowy at the other end of the long, narrow room'.

Though Heyst never desires Lena, she attracts Ricardo as she had

attracted Schomberg. Ricardo's instinctive violence is barely suppressed and only held in subjection by the rational influence of Jones;
and his passion contrasts with Jones' passivity and apathy just as
Lena's contrasts with Heyst's. Ricardo recognizes their similarities,
for both have their origins in the dregs of mankind and both are
precariously dependent upon gentlemen with strange sexual habits.

The sexual relationship of Lena and Ricardo reveals aspects of
their characters that are repressed in their liaisons with Heyst and
Jones. When Ricardo emphasizes their common background,
attacks their gentlemen and undermines Lena's fragile security, he is
trying to convince her that he can give her what Heyst has failed to
provide. He wants to display, not hide Lena, and naïvely asks her to
call him 'husband'. Though Ricardo increases Lena's doubts about
Heyst, he also intensifies her guilt and her craving for sacrifice and
redemption.

Since the passionate Lena is a 'bad girl' with considerable sexual
experience and Heyst is clearly unable to satisfy her emotional or
physical needs, she subconsciously responds to Ricardo's sexual
assault. Yet it is obvious that if Lena is to remain the redemptive
heroine and achieve the ironic victory, she cannot actually be raped
by Ricardo. Just as we realize that Davidson could not possibly
know what he is narrating and that Ricardo would not really speak as
he does in the novel, so we are also aware that the rape scene would
not actually take place as Conrad describes it. Though he overtly
portrays a conventional scene in which the heroine defeats the
villain, he also covertly yet unmistakably suggests an alternative —
and more convincing — reality.

There is considerable evidence to suggest that Ricardo's attempted
rape has upon Lena the psychological and emotional effect of an
actual rape and that she derives a certain satisfaction from his violent
attack. Despite Conrad's explanations, it is impossible to believe that
Lena could successfully resist the surprise attack of the armed
Ricardo; and her 'fingers like steel' and 'muscles like a giant' are a
startling contrast to the frail and frightened Lena of Sourabaya, with
her 'slender white bust' and prettily crossed feet. Ricardo's assault
and her complicity in his escape lead to an unusual bond of intimacy
between them. He believes 'A woman that does not make a noise
after an attempt of that kind has tacitly condoned the offence', and he
talks to her tenderly, as if they had slept together. He has, in fact,

torn open her sarong and seen her naked body, and his 'sudden relaxation of the terrific hug' leaves him 'crestfallen', like a cock after treading.

Finally, Ricardo's knife is an obvious symbol of his penis. He boasts 'I carry a pretty deadly thing about me' and Lena remarks that he could rape her only 'with that thing stuck in my side'. When Lena disobeys Heyst and secretly meets Ricardo in the evening, the phallic connotations of the bone-handled weapon become glaring: 'a terror of impatience to clutch the frightful thing, glimpsed once and unforgettable, agitated her hands'. Lena symbolically consummates her sexual combat with Ricardo when she seductively steals his knife: 'she let it slip into the fold of her dress, and laid her forearms with clasped fingers over her knees, which she pressed desperately together. The dreaded thing was out of sight at last. She felt a dampness break out all over her' (319).

Though Ricardo is sick of crawling on his belly for Jones and wants to free himself from his master's sexual domination, he gets perverse pleasure from debasing himself before Lena and makes the paradoxical but revealing statement about his own fantasies: 'What you want is a man, a master that will let you put the heel of your shoe on his neck.' Ricardo's mastery consists of persuading Lena to satisfy his masochistic urges. He substitutes foot-fetishism for sexual intercourse and tells Lena that he is 'as tired as if I had been pouring my life-blood here on these planks for you to dabble your white feet in'. When Ricardo surrenders his knife he demands her foot, and as she slowly brings it out from under her dress he throws himself on it greedily and 'clasping her ankle, pressed his lips time after time to the instep, muttering gasping words that were like sobs, making little noises that resembled the sounds of grief and distress' (320).

Ricardo's assault on Lena illuminates her unhappy relationship with Heyst as well as Ricardo's connection with Jones. Though Ricardo's violent lust for Lena is an ironic reflection of Heyst's sexual failure, he achieves orgasm with Lena in a fashion that is as perverse as his homosexual acts with Jones. All three men (as well as Schomberg and Wang) share a common misogyny, which is manifested in Heyst's impotence, Jones' homosexuality and Ricardo's exhibitionism, voyeurism and fetishism.[13].

Ricardo's relationship with Jones, as everyone immediately notices, is scarcely secretarial. Ricardo admits that Jones 'seemed to touch me inside somewhere', and at the first opportunity he attaches himself to his Governor and becomes, as Jones salaciously boasts to Heyst, 'absolutely identified with all my ideas, wishes, and even whims'. Though Ricardo is Jones' paid lover he has the 'morals of a cat', and the marks on his face suggest the great as well as the small pox. Ricardo enjoys deceiving Jones, having furtive little flings (which never amount to anything and are therefore tolerated by Jones), and attempting to excite himself and confirm his masculinity by making sexual overtures to women, like Lena, whom he threatens with violence but is actually afraid to sleep with:

> Once I was courting a girl. I used to kiss her behind the ear and say to myself: 'If you only knew who's kissing you, my dear, you would scream and bolt!' Ha! ha! Not that I wanted to do them any harm; but I felt the power in myself. (115)

Conrad is most explicit about the sexual anomalies of the handsome and shrill-voice Jones, an invalid who dies in his gorgeous blue silk dressing-gown. Jones has a violent and passionate hatred of women, and his obviously feminine eyelashes and waspish pencilled eyebrows make him appear 'unnatural', 'vicious', 'depraved' and 'disgusting'. In Mexico Jones picked up ragged and bare-legged street urchins for his pleasure, and the brazen girls asked Ricardo 'if the English *caballero* in the *posada* was a monk in disguise, or if he has taken a vow to the *sanctissima madre* not to speak to a woman, or whether — you can imagine what fairly free-spoken girls will ask' (138).

Conrad's portrayal of Jones and Heyst has been criticized by Guerard, who has not recognized the significance of their final encounter. He writes that Jones 'seeks to paralyze Heyst by insisting that they have much in common. Yet this scene, using again one of Conrad's most striking psychological intuitions, seems untrue or at least unimportant . . . The only genuine identification in *Victory* would connect Heyst's diffidence with Mr. Jones' "horror of feminine presence"'.[14] But during Heyst's confrontations with Jones — which parallel the previous encounters of Heyst and Lena, Lena and Ricardo, and lead directly to the tragic climax of the novel — Jones confirms Schomberg's accusations and Lena's suspicions by recognizing the homosexual element in Heyst that has led to his fear of women, his guilt and his impotence. Though Jones never directly accuses Heyst of homosexuality, he enjoys implicating his victim in his own corruption and stresses the similarities between himself and his secret sharer.

Jones complains bitterly to Heyst that he was hounded out of society by a lot of highly moral souls and states that his presence on the island is no more morally reprehensible than Heyst's: 'Something has driven you out [too] — the originality of your ideas, perhaps. Or your *tastes*.' And in their final meeting Jones insists that he has remained closer to his origins, breeding and traditions than Heyst: 'Not everyone can divest himself of the prejudices of a gentleman as easily as you have done.' Though Jones knows nothing of Heyst except the malicious gossip he has heard indirectly from Schomberg via Ricardo, he is able to wound Heyst with insinuations that awaken his guilt about Morrison. Jones considers himself more open and honest than Heyst because he admits his homosexuality instead of trying to repress and deny it, and preys on the world instead of evading it. Jones carries the philosophy of Heyst's father (who also wore 'an ample blue dressing-gown') to the logical extreme of negation. For just as Heyst (like his father) believes that men are evil and the earth is 'the appointed hatching planet of calumny enough to furnish the whole universe', so Jones believes he is justified in exacting retribution through ferocity and violence.

While Ricardo is pursuing his masochistic gratifications, Heyst awakens Jones' doubts about his faithful secretary just as Ricardo had stirred Lena's suspicions of Heyst, and Jones discovers that the well-groomed Ricardo (who has recently become concerned with his appearance) has been deceiving him with Lena. In a rage of jealousy and disgust Jones rushes out to murder Ricardo and finds him kissing Lena's feet. At that fatal moment, when Jones aims at his lover and shoots Lena, Heyst becomes painfully aware of his sexual failures and is convinced that Lena has deceived him.

When the dying Lena insists 'I would never, never have let him . . . get it back', even if she had to stab Ricardo, she reiterates the thematic connection between loving and killing. Heyst repeats that though women have their own weapon (guile), he has been a 'disarmed' (impotent) man all his life. Then, in a moment of sudden fury, Heyst seems to recognize Lena's corporality for the first time and to re-enact Ricardo's assault: he 'started tearing open the front of the girl's dress' and staring at the 'little black hole', made by the bullet, beneath her swelling breast.[15] Lena's sexual excitement during her morbid consummation with Heyst accounts for her swelling breast as the blood flows from her wound, and she clasps Ricardo's knife 'like a child reaching eagerly for a toy'. Despite his final 'thematic' pronouncement, Heyst never abandons the idea that 'he who forms a tie is lost'; and his inability to grant Lena's dying wish to take her in his arms — even as a formal gesture of consolation — confirms the emptiness of her thoroughly ironic victory. Moser is therefore inaccurate when he states that in the final scene Conrad fails to show the intended meaning of the novel: 'Lena defeating the evil of the world',[16] for as the villains kill each other Heyst is agonized by his impotence and his guilt about Lena's meaningless sacrifice. He 'couldn't stand his thoughts before her dead body' and attempts to punish and purify himself by a fiery death.

Homosexuality, though rarely made explicit, has an important function in *Victory*. The clever, witty, depraved Jones is a classic homosexual villain who is guilty of murder and theft as well as sexual corruption. But Heyst's repressed homosexuality and impotence symbolize in sexual terms the conflict between his desire for isolation and need for love. His relationship with Lena (who is also called Alma) represents a spiritual as well as a sexual struggle, for she is trying to save him not from death, but from a kind of death-in-life that is the tragic legacy of his father's philosophy. The great strength of Conrad's underrated novel is his use of the homosexual theme to portray Heyst's emotional sterility and denial of life. Heyst's failure to respond to Lena's love after his first generous impulse leads to the victory of pessimism and negation over devotion and sacrifice.

VII

FORSTER

A Room With A View, Maurice, The Life to Come

Forster's novels had their intellectual origin in the pervasively homosexual milieu of *fin de siècle* Cambridge, an atmosphere (described in Holroyd's *Lytton Strachey*) in which dons like Goldsworthy Lowes Dickinson and John McTaggart, a dominant influence on Forster and his circle of friends, practised and preached the Greek ideal of male love. Almost all of Forster's fiction concerns an attempt to make the emotional leap from repression to fulfilment, and achieve a triumph of the intuitive and impulsive over the rational and repressive mode of experience. If Forster's work is viewed as a consistent whole rather than as separate entities, it is possible to see a recurrent pattern of latent homosexual relationships. The friendships of Eustace and Gennaro in 'The Story of a Panic' (1904), Philip and Gino in *Where Angels Fear to Tread* (1905) and Rickie and Stephen in *The Longest Journey* (1907) culminate with Beebe and George in *A Room With A View* (1908). In the Italian novels male love is disguised as a temptation to intimacy, and the homosexual theme does not surface until his posthumous works, *Maurice* (1971) and *The Life to Come* (1972).

Where Angels Fear to Tread foreshadows *A Room With A View* just as *The Longest Journey* prefigures *Maurice*. Gino's temptation of Philip, who distrusts emotion, is subtle and complex, for both men have a homosexual element in their nature, and their sado-masochistic connection builds up to a crescendo of pain through a series of hints and touches: 'Though you become as David and Jonathan, you need never enter his home, nor he yours'. After his marriage to Lilia, Gino agrees with his friend Spiridione: 'Sono poco simpatiche le donne. And the time we waste over them is much'.

When Forster describes Gino's procreative 'desire that his son should be like him, and should have sons like him, to people the earth', he calls this the 'strongest desire that can come to a man' and then adds the revealing qualification — 'if it comes to him at all'. At the opera Philip is enchanted by the light caress of Carella's arm across his back; in the café Gino lays a sympathetic hand on Philip's knee; when Philip tells Gino of the baby's death he touches him on the shoulder for consolation; and when Gino twists his arm and he strikes Gino down, Philip passes his arm around him and is filled with pity and tenderness. Philip tells Caroline that after the baby's funeral Gino nursed him, for 'I was the only person he had to be kind to'. He is bound to Gino 'by ties of almost alarming intimacy' and confesses, 'I love him too!'[1]

The characters and themes of *Where Angels Fear to Tread* are repeated three years later in *A Room With A View*, where Gino becomes George, Philip is Cecil, Caroline is Lucy and Harriet is Charlotte. In the later novel, however, George and Lucy achieve a kind of fulfilment in love that is denied to Philip and Caroline.

I. A ROOM WITH A VIEW

Like *Howards End*, *A Room With A View* is structured by a series of contrasting characters, settings and values which heighten the dramatic tension and enforce the theme. In the first novel the Schlegel-Wilcox opposition suggests a number of thematic polarities: feminine-masculine, culture-business, socialism-capitalism, country-city, tradition-change, private-public, intuition-calculation, homes-houses. In *A Room With A View* there are similar polarities: Emerson-Eager, George-Cecil, Lucy-Charlotte, Mrs Honeychurch-Mrs Vyse; Italy-England, Surrey-London; and classical-medieval, passion-intellect, instinct-convention, truth-lies, outdoor-indoor, sunlight-shadow. The views, music and violets are symbols of the first group while snobbery, hypocrisy and repression define the second.[2]

The one major character who does not fit into this somewhat schematic pattern is the Reverend Beebe, who unlike the other 'fixed' characters, begins in the vital first group, changes radically and unexpectedly, and ends in the second rather morbid group. The interpretation of Beebe's character represents a central critical question in the novel.[3] Beebe is first presented in an entirely sympathetic light. He gently explains to Lucy and Charlotte the disinterested motives of the eccentric Mr Emerson and smooths the way for Lucy to accept the room with a view. He is associated with music and pleasant memories, suggests a fine outing, and is so liberal and enlightened, so tolerant, sympathetic and good-natured (in contrast to the pompous and priggish snob Reverend Eager) that Lucy happily exclaims, 'No one would take him for a clergyman'.[4] The least attractive aspect of Beebe's personality is his peculiar attitude toward women. 'Girls like Lucy were charming to look at, but Mr Beebe was, from rather profound reasons, somewhat chilly in his attitude towards the other sex, and preferred to be interested rather than enthralled' (38), and when Charlotte irritated him at the *Pensione* he inwardly cursed the female sex. He tells Freddy in his ambiguous 'funny way, when you never quite know what he means . . . "Mr Vyse is an ideal bachelor . . . he's like me — better detached" ' (91), and Charlotte complains that neither Beebe nor Eager is a 'real man' (83).

The 'Twelfth Chapter' (which like the central 'Fourth Chapter' in Part I has no descriptive title) contains the naked bathing scene whose strong homosexual overtones explain Beebe's character. Before the swim begins Beebe gives a thinly veiled plea for homosexual love by categorically stating, 'We despise the body less than women do. But not until we are comrades shall we enter the garden' of Eden (134). This is a dominant idea of Walt Whitman, whose considerable influence on Forster (and on D. H. Lawrence) goes far beyond 'Passage to India'. As Lawrence writes of Whitman: 'The strange calamus has its pink-tinged root by the pond, and it sends up its leaves of comradeship, comrades from one root, without the intervention of woman, the female. So he sings of this mystery of manly love, the love of comrades. Over and over he says the same thing. the new world will be built on the love of comrades.'[5] An interesting analogue for Forster's bathing scene is the eleventh 'sexion' of Whitman's 'Song of Myself' in which the twenty-eight naked men, exposing their parts in the sun, are entirely self-contained and completely indifferent to the woman's passionate desires.

Which of the young men does she like best?
Ah the homeliest of them is beautiful to her.

Where are you off to, lady? for I see you,
You splash in the water there, yet stay stock still in your room.

Dancing and laughing along the beach came the twenty-ninth
    bather,
The rest did not see her, but she saw them and loved them.

The beards of the young men glisten'd with wet, it ran from their
    long hair,

Little streams pass'd all over their bodies.
An unseen hand also pass'd over their bodies,
It descended tremblingly from their temples and ribs.

The young men float on their backs, their white bellies bulge to
    the sun, they do not ask who seizes fast to them,
They do not know who puffs and declines with pending and
    bending arch,
They do not think whom they souse with spray.

In Forster's swimming scene George and Beebe respond to Freddy
Honeychurch's 'Come and have a bathe' and accompany him to the
same pond where Lucy used to swim until she was discovered by the
officious Charlotte (who later discovers her kissing George). Lucy
was frigidly kissed by Cecil (the third of four symbolic kisses in the
novel) at this pond, where Cecil recast that emotional failure in his
imagination. Beebe first decides not to swim and rather ecstatically
observes the two young men undress — 'Mr Beebe watched them,
and watched the seeds of the willow-herb dance chorically above
their heads' (138) — as Forster hellenizes nature to blend with the
classical ideal of manly love. Freddy plunges in immediately, but
George hesitates, heroically 'Michelangelesque on the flooded
margin', until the bank breaks away and he too falls into the pool.
(When Lucy falls into the violets to receive George's first kiss, a scene
described entirely in water metaphors, the ground also gave way
beneath her, so that these two crucial scenes are subtly linked.)
    Beebe, his blood stirred by their youthful enthusiasm and the
wonder of the water, now strips off, enters the pool with the boys,
and becomes transformed. Suffused with youthful spirits, he

abandons his dignity and joins Freddy as George 'smiled, flung himself at them, splashed them, ducked them, kicked them, muddied them, and drove them out of the pool' (139). He races around the pond after them, remonstrates as they toss around his clerical garb, and regaining control of himself, warns them that people are coming and jumps back into the pool which contains his floating underwear. But his warning goes unheeded as Freddy and George, in a wonderfully comic confrontation, run stark naked into Mrs Honeychurch, Cecil and Lucy.[6] Only Cecil is seriously disturbed; the others are merely startled and amused.

The effect of this bathing scene, which cements the friendship of Freddy and George, and releases George from his serious depression, also has an enduring influence on Mr Beebe. This is ironically described in ecclesiastical imagery: 'It had been a call to the blood and to the relaxed will, a passing benediction whose influence did not pass, a holiness, a spell, a momentary chalice for youth' (141). Beebe's latent homosexuality has been released and he has fallen in love with George, and this will determine his behaviour throughout the rest of the novel.

Bathing scenes in Forster's fiction are either a symbolic release from sexual inhibitions or a manifestation of sexual repression. In 'The Point of It', a story with strong homosexual overtones, Micky and Harold 'had rowed out to the dunes at the slack, bathed, raced, eaten, slept, bathed and raced and eaten again. Micky was in roaring spirits'.[7] In *Howards End* Charles Wilcox and his friend Albert Fussell, with considerably less abandon, go for a morning dip at Oniton followed by servants carrying their bathing costumes. Margaret Schlegel observes their contretemps with amusement and her spontaneity is contrasted with their paralysis, for the 'athletes' run away from the life of the body as soon as they hear her voice.[8] And Forster writes that in a cancelled 'fantasy-chapter' of *The Longest Journey*, Stephen bathes in a river near a railway bridge and a passing engine-driver 'abuses him in the filthiest language for wearing no costume. The same thing once happened to my friend Lowes Dickinson',[9] 'whose opinions on sex ran contrary to Christian ethics'.[10]

Just as Beebe 'was conscious of some bitter disappointment' (100) when he learned that Lucy and Cecil were going to marry, so he was pleased when their engagement was broken off.

His belief in celibacy, so reticent, so carefully concealed beneath his tolerance and culture, now came to the surface and expanded like some delicate flower. 'They that marry do well, but they that refrain do better.'[11] So ran his belief, and he never heard that an engagement was broken off but with a slight feeling of pleasure.

Though Forster comments that this 'very subtle and quite undogmatic' feeling 'explains his action subsequently' (199), Beebe's very reticence and careful concealment suggest that his views on celibacy are based on personal preference rather than on Pauline doctrine. A fundamental questioning of the value of heterosexual love is recurrent in Forster's works.

When Margaret Schlegel discovers that Jackie Bast was once Henry Wilcox's mistress, she asks herself: 'Are the sexes really races, each with its own code of morality, and their mutual love a mere device of Nature to keep things going? Strip human intercourse of the proprieties, and is it reduced to this?'[12] In *A Passage to India* Adela's frightening fantasy in the cave emphasizes the dangerous and threatening aspects of sexuality. The weary and disillusioned Mrs Moore asks (alluding to the idea in Plato's *Symposium* of an original. single sex that split apart): 'Why all this marriage, marriage? . . . The human race would have become a single person centuries ago if marriage was any use. And all this rubbish about love, love in a church, love in a cave, as if there is the least difference.'[13] Even Fielding, Forster's most attractive hero, dislikes children, is cynical about marriage and says, 'I no longer want love'.[14] The incident of Fielding's lost collar stud and his passionate defence of Aziz suggest an intimacy that is never developed in the novel; and though he marries Mrs Moore's daughter Stella, his marriage, like that of all the English, is disappointing. Aziz is a widower, Mrs Moore a widow, Adela a spinster, Ronny a bachelor and McBryde an adulterer, and a similar pattern is found in all of Forster's fiction.

'The Curate's Friend' (1907), a story published the year before *A Room With A View*, bears some interesting similarities to the theme of that novel. Like Beebe, whose 'chief pleasure [was] to provide people with happy memories' (43), the curate is 'one whose happiness consists in giving happiness to others'. Neither clergyman understands heterosexual love, 'the mystery of love of the eternal man and the eternal woman';[15] and bathing occurs significantly in both works. The curate is first angered when his fiancée, with a Faun's help, falls in love with another man, but he is soon joyous and relieved when he escapes from conventional marriage and sex. The story ends with a curious confession as the curate says: 'If I breathed one word of that [joy], my present life, so agreeable and profitable, would come to an end, my congregation would depart, and so should I, and instead of being an asset to my parish, I might find myself an expense to the nation',[16] an expense not as an indigent, but as a prisoner. Stone is certainly right when he says the story 'is a covert love poem, and the spirit of that love is illicit'.[17] Forster wrote what are probably his sincerest views on love in a letter to T. E. Lawrence: 'I think of a remark of mine which you once approved . . . It was about love, how over-rated and over-written it is, and how the relation one would like between people is a mixture of friendliness and lust.'[18]

It is precisely this negative strain in Forster's works (something quite different from Whitman) that undermines his power and effectiveness as a novelist and accounts for the spinsterish and effete quality that sometimes obtrudes in his fiction. This anti-vital aspect of Beebe's personality is subtly (and not entirely unsympathetically) portrayed when, just after stating his views on celibacy, he returns to Windy Corner to find Lucy playing the piano and singing a song from Scott's *The Bride of Lammermoor* (1819) that Cecil gave her:

> Look not thou on beauty's charming,
> Sit thou still when kings are arming,
> Taste not when the wine-cup glistens,
> Speak not when the people listens,
> Stop thine ear against the singer,
> From the red gold keep thy finger,
> Vacant heart and hand and eye,
> Easy live and quiet die. (200-2)

Beebe approves of this song, which describes the emotionally sterile 'medieval' lives of Charlotte, Eager, Cecil and himself, and represents a profane variation of St Paul's idea of renunciation and celibacy. As Beebe asks himself: 'Why should Lucy want either to *marry* or to travel when she had such friends at home?' and he states 'It's a beautiful song and a wise one' (201). The idea in this song is directly opposed to the theme of the Housman poem that Mr

Emerson, who believes that Cecil's attitude toward women has 'kept Europe back for a thousand years' (177), begins to quote earlier in the novel (32), for the second (omitted) quatrain encourages a spontaneous response to life:

> Take my hand quick and tell me,
> What have you in your heart.

The connection between Lucy and Beebe, and the ambivalent strains in their characters that pull them toward life and away from it, are reflected in their names: Honeychurch and *Bee*be. Honey suggests sweetness, Lucy suggests light, and both suggest the bees in 'The Battle of the Books' who have 'chosen to fill our Hives with Honey and Wax, thus furnishing Mankind with the two Noblest of Things, which are Sweetness and Light'.[19]

The *church* in Forster's novel stands opposed to these values, and beneath the sign of the Beehive Tavern — 'a beehive trimmed evenly with bees' (199) — The Reverend Beebe plots with Charlotte to keep Lucy from the 'temptation' of marriage. In this important scene, Forster brilliantly connects Beebe with bees by alluding to the most famous apian reference in the Classics — Virgil's fourth *Georgic* — in which they are associated with both asceticism and religion:

> But veriest marvel of the ways of bees
> Is that their limbs mix not in love's embrace
> Not weaken them by lust, nor ever bear
> Their young in pangs of travail . . .
>
> These acts and powers observing, some declare
> That bees have portion in the mind of God
> And life from heaven derive.[20]

The 'weaken limbs by lust' is a classical equivalent of Paul's warning in Romans 7:23: 'I see another law in my members, warring against the law of my mind, and bringing me into captivity to the law of sin which is in my members'.

Like the bees in *A Passage to India* who painfully sting Ralph Moore after an Indian has pronounced, 'They will not hurt us, whose lives are chaste',[21] Beebe, though apparently harmless, is actually dangerous. He pretends at first to be on the side of sweetness and light, remains neutral in the Phaeton-Persephone dispute, and ultimately reveals himself not as a 'bee' but as a *black* 'spider' who 'lives in a web of petty secrets' (196).

At the end of the novel Lucy rejects Beebe's doctrines, and as she realizes her love for George the 'water-tight compartments' break down and music and life mingle within her. She is inspired by Mr Emerson's central speech on love and passion that forms an ironic counterpoint to 'Mr Beebe's voice running through the litany to a minute congregation' (209), for Lucy had refused to attend saying 'No *church* for me'. Beebe, who could not acknowledge passion, is characteristically distracted by his old mother at the crucial moment of Lucy's self-discovery. Beebe's 'white face, with its ruddy whiskers, seemed suddenly inhuman. A long black column' in clerical dress, he finally aligns himself with the forces of bitterness and darkness. He tells Lucy in a low stern voice that her engagement is a personal tragedy for him: 'I am more grieved than I can possibly express. It is lamentable, lamentable — incredible.' He declares that George 'no longer interests me' (that is, as a possible lover), and they hear him, a devoted only child, 'guiding his mother up-stairs' (217).

There are some important parallels in Forster's novels for Beebe's *gran rifiuto*. Stone has shown that Beebe's 'tone is exactly that of Dickinson on the occasion of [Roger] Fry's marriage',[22] and he mentions Dickinson's connection with the cancelled naked bathing scene in *The Longest Journey*. Helen Schlegel's horrified response to the news of Margaret's engagement to Henry Wilcox, though certainly more reasonable than Beebe's, has the same petulant and querulous tone that comes (at least in part) from a similar destructive jealousy: ' "Don't, don't do such a thing! I tell you not to — don't. I know — don't . . . Panic and emptiness", sobbed Helen. "Don't." '[23] A much closer parallel — between the lovers and the response to their engagement — appears in *The Longest Journey*, which was published the year before *A Room With A View*. Rickie and Agnes first kiss in a dell that is similar to the violet-covered hillside where, directed by Phaeton, Lucy first kisses George — both are described in water imagery and both have a view and mythological associations;[24] and Rickie puts his head on Agnes' lap just as George does on his honeymoon. And the bitter tone of Ansell's (more justified) response to Rickie's engagement is similar to Beebe's: 'Will either of these happinesses last? His can't. Hers only for a time. I fight this woman not only because she fights me, but because I foresee the most appalling catastrophe.'[25]

Just as from 'rather profound' homosexual reasons Beebe was merely 'interested' in young girls and lost interest in them as soon as they ceased to be purely aesthetic objects and developed an emotional and sexual life of their own, so George 'no longer interests' Beebe when he too commits himself to marriage and heterosexual love. As Lucy significantly says on her honeymoon, 'He will never forgive us — I mean, he will never be interested in us again' (221). In short, Beebe cannot forgive the lovers for acknowledging passion, for choosing life, for doing what he himself cannot do, for 'betraying' him. The central paradox of the novel is that although Beebe is portrayed negatively at the end, we know from Forster's other works that he is essentially sympathetic to Beebe's views on celibacy and sex. Since Forster was unwilling or unable (in 1908) to endorse homosexual love directly, he was forced to present his views obliquely and ambiguously,[26] to deflect them through a clerical guise, so that our response to Beebe is ambivalent. It is essential to recognize that Beebe's character and beliefs qualify and question what appears to be the only romantic and happy ending in Forster's fiction.[27]

II. MAURICE

'The sun burns on the half-mown hill,
    By now the blood is dried;
And Maurice amongst the hay lies still
    And my knife is in his side.'

A. E. Housman, *A Shropshire Lad* (VIII)

Maurice, which concerns a different kind of pastoral penetration, was written in 1913-14, between *Howards End* and *A Passage to India*, when Forster was at the height of his creative powers. But Forster refused to publish the novel in his lifetime and expose his private self, even after the Sexual Offences Act of 1967 had legalized homosexuality between consenting adults. And when *Maurice* appeared posthumously in 1971 it had lost all its moral and social significance. This artistic failure clarifies our understanding of the homosexual themes in the earlier novels and allows an insight into an obscure aspect of Forster's life.

The plot is simple — too simple. The eponymous hero, Maurice Hall, 'bourgeois, unfinished and stupid' (unlike Forster) is brought up in a family of females and in a home that 'emasculated everything', and moves through second-rate prep and public schools to an inspiring life at Cambridge (somewhat as Forster did). In the course of his self-discovery he experiences a series of exemplary episodes that crudely signal their message, like a ship in distress: a hypocritical lecture on sex, a dream of a naked boy, the omission of an obscene reference in a Greek lesson, a gauche failure with a girl, an unjust academic punishment.

At Cambridge Maurice first learns to recognize his true nature, responds to the homosexual overtures of Clive Durham and enters into a purely platonic relationship with him. But Forster's portrayal of the emotions of love at the most significant moments in the novel is disastrously false and hysterical:

> Then savage, reckless, drenched with the rain, he saw in the first glimmer of dawn the window of Durham's room, and his heart leapt alive and shook him to pieces. It cried, 'You love and are loved.' He looked round the court. It cried, 'You are strong, he weak and alone,' won over his will. Terrified at what he must do, the caught hold of the mullion and sprang.
> 'Maurice —'
> As he alighted his name had been called out of dreams[28]

— not out of reality. Both Maurice and Clive have uncomfortable relationships with their mothers (their fathers are dead) and fancy themselves misogynists. Maurice selfishly admits, 'No one except his mother mattered and she only a little';[29] and Clive's mother, whose dower house suffers appropriately from bad drains, uses this anal symbol as an excuse to reside with him permanently.

While travelling in Greece, quite suddenly and without warning, Clive reverts to heterosexuality in 'a blind alteration of the life spirit' and writes Maurice: 'Against my will I have become normal. I cannot help it.' This is, of course, an ironic reversal of the traditional Forsterian plot, for the combination of Mediterranean sun and platonic philosophy usually liberates the latent homosexuality of his characters. Soon afterwards Clive marries, and Maurice, after suffering loneliness, pain and guilt, makes abortive attempts to return to normality through a futile confession to the family doctor (his surrogate father) and some unsuccessful sessions with a quack hypnotist — the only available options, Forster suggests, for 'an unspeakable of the Oscar Wilde sort'.

Then, while visiting Clive's country house, Maurice first experiences physical passion with Clive's gamekeeper, Alec Scudder, 'an untamed son of the woods'. After some initial distrust they confess their mutual love, Maurice gives up his stockbroking job and Alec his plans to emigrate, and they go off to live in the greenwood (as Clive has gone off with Anne Woods) with every promise of happiness.

There are a number of crucial weaknesses in this very tame ('He was lovely to be with . . . the longed-for dream') and very dated ('I say, will you kiss me?') novel, and the inevitable reaction of anyone who had waited more than fifty years to read it must have been serious disappointment. There are no interesting characters in the book, for Maurice is a philistine youth surrounded by a thinly sketched cast of consummately dull mediocrities. Forster neither analyses Maurice's homosexuality, nor explains why Clive becomes normal. Maurice and Alec, as Lytton Strachey pointed out in 1915, have nothing in common but curiosity and lust, and their happy ending is totally improbable. Forster intended Maurice and Alec to have 'the fullest possible knowledge of each other' but their puerile passions remain shallow and sentimental. Maurice asks, 'Did you ever dream you'd a friend, Alec? Nothing else but just "my friend," he trying to help you and you him. "A friend," he repeated.' And Alec replies in a mawkish letter: 'Dear Sir, let me share with you once before leaving Old England if it is not asking too much. I have key, will let you in . . . I since cricket match do long to talk with one of my arms round you, then place both arms round you and share with you, the above now seems sweeter to me than words can say' (192). As Edward Carpenter writes in *The Intermediate Sex*, 'One may safely say that the defect of the male Uranian, or Urning, is *not* sensuality — but rather *sentimentality*'.[30]

Maurice, unlike Forster's other fiction, is a *roman à thèse* whose aim is to defend homosexual love (from beyond the grave) and show it could be successful. Forster felt a 'happy ending was imperative' and admits that he was overwhelmed by the temptation 'to grant one's creations a happiness actual life does not supply'.[31] His failure in this respect — and his doctrinaire premises made failure inevitable — is the novel's most serious weakness, for neither the arguments nor the emotions are rendered convincingly. Both Clive and Maurice approach homosexuality as an Hellenic predilection — 'The Greeks, or most of them, were that way inclined and to omit it is to omit the mainstay of Athenian society' — and argue that men can experience a nobler, deeper 'harmony of body and soul that I don't think women have even guessed'. These ideas (and 'mainstay' indicates the bias about a harmony of body and soul that is *not* achieved by any of the characters in the novel) were expounded in *The Greek Way of Life* (1898) by Goldsworthy Lowes Dickinson, whose influence on his biographer Forster is incalculable and who, with Walt Whitman and Edward Carpenter, made up a trinity of public apologists for homosexuality.[32]

It is fascinating to follow the various ways in which Forster attempts to justify homosexuals, whom he portrays (fairly) as martyrs to the law and (jesuitically) as perfectly normal 'except on one point' — since that is the point of the novel. David and Jonathan and 'the disciple that Jesus loved' (John 16:26) provide familiar Scriptural support. Tchaikovsky, composer of the 'Symphonie Incestueuse et Pathétique', who fell in love with his nephew and dedicated his masterpiece to him, represents an artistic model. But the most unusual, if not the most convincing argument, is that the invert, because of his dualistic incorporation of male and female characteristics, has a heightened sensibility and a more profound aesthetic understanding:

> Look at that picture [by Michelangelo], for instance. I love it because, like the painter himself, I love the subject. I don't judge it with eyes of the normal man. There seem two roads for arriving at Beauty — one is in common, and all the world has reached Michelangelo by it, but the other is private to me and a few more. We come to him by both roads. On the other hand Greuze — his subject matter repels me. (83)

Apart from the fact that Michelangelo (the most famous homosexual painter) is in no way comparable to the rather banal — and cuckolded — Greuze (whose paintings are later found in the doctor's house), this snobbish passage, with its appeal to the precious few, confuses emotional enthusiasm for the *subject* with aesthetic perception of the painting.

The book is particularly weak when Forster attempts to introduce social as well as sexual themes. Maurice's concern about the 'shocking' treatment of servants (i.e. Alec) is seriously vitiated by his sexual and economic exploitation of the gamekeeper, for he can achieve sexual satisfaction only when he uses money to liberate himself from the rigid restrictions of his class. And Alec's attempt at blackmail (instigated by his 'bad' brother) is too feeble to be convincing.

Forster takes an extremely deterministic view of homosexuality and tends to blame society (he had 'been fed upon lies') for problems that are partially due to Maurice's lack of self-insight and moral courage. Forster tries to invest Maurice with a spurious heroism by having him announce, 'Two men can defy the world', but his retreat to the greenwood is a fanciful attempt to *escape* from the world.

But the novel is not entirely without merit. Forster, obviously dissatisfied with it, revised the work in 1919, 1932 and again in 1960, and gave it an ironic and balanced structure. Clive's first declaration of love, which leaves Maurice scandalized and horrified (the irony is rather heavy-handed at this point), is echoed when Maurice announces his love for Alec, the servant-substitute, to a depressed and offended Clive. And Alec, in response to a resonant though ambiguous 'Come!', climbs through Maurice's window (he happens to be near a ladder when called) just as Maurice had entered Clive's.

The most potentially interesting moments in the novel are, unfortunately, hinted at rather than developed, almost as if Forster were so eager to reach his happy ending that he could not pause for long en route. There is a clever but brief portrait of Lytton Strachey as Risley, a flagrant homosexual whose cynical and defiant temperament contrasts with Maurice's timid and repressed personality. Maurice accuses his attractive sister of 'corrupting' his lover, but the psychological implications of this 'incestuous jealousy' are never discussed and the incident ends with a characteristic fit of petulance. And Maurice's half-hearted but guilt-ridden attempt to seduce his houseguest, the schoolboy Dickie, who has the callous but pragmatic attitude of an attractive fag toward a powerful prefect — 'If Hall insisted, he would not kick up a row, but he had rather not' — could have been a meaningful portrayal of the conflict between morality and lust.

Lytton Strachey censured Forster's oblique references to masturbation and rightly objected, 'I really think the whole conception of male copulation in the book is rather diseased — in fact morbid and unnatural . . . A propos of Maurice tossing himself off (you call it a 'malpractice') (Ch. xxxii), you say — "He knew what the price would be — a creeping apathy towards all things." How did Maurice know that? And how do you? Surely the truth is that as often as not the effects are simply nil.'[33] Forster may have picked up his clinical notion about masturbation from Walt Whitman, who 'speaks of the ashen grey faces of onanists: the faded colours, the puffy features and the unwholesome complexion of the professed pederast with his peculiar cachectic expression, indescribable but once seen never forgotten, stamp the breed'.[34] Though Forster revised this passage, which was omitted from the final version of the novel, it is still not very satisfactory. At school Maurice suffered from onanistic exhaustion and 'desisted from these [acts] after the novelty was over, finding that they brought him more fatigue than pleasure'. When he returned to masturbation after being abandoned by Clive, he 'found it did bring him a degraded kind of peace' — a marginal improvement over 'creeping apathy'. Finally, Maurice achieves considerable masochistic pleasure by cleaning up the close-stool after Clive's attacks of diarrhoea. There is always an element of degradation and self-punishment in Forster's homosexual attractions (Gino twisting Philip's broken arm in *Where Angels Fear to Tread*), and Maurice's connection with Clive's 'filth' is the symbolic equivalent of the 'self-condemned feeling' that impels Maurice toward a lower-class lover, with whom sex replaces shit.

The themes of the novel — how to live frankly, the connection between love and lust (that so troubled Mrs Moore), the exposed heart and deepened vision that makes the armies of humanity come alive — are familiarly Forsterian. The superficial characterization of *Maurice* is rather like the early stories, especially the Eustace-Gennaro relationship in 'The Story of a Panic', and its homosexual theme has affinities with *A Room With A View*.

But in plot, characters and theme it is most closely related to *The Longest Journey*. There are the coincidental meetings and sudden alterations, the hypocrisy of public school and parson, the usefulness of the working class and idleness of the upper, the worship of nature and fear of urban blight, the longing for Greece and Italy, the ambiguous boyish ragging, the inevitable nude bathing scenes where one man passively observes the other, the awkwardness of clothes on young bodies, the ironic paraphrase of biblical language, and the witty and aphoristic style. More specifically, in both *Maurice* and *The Longest Journey*, the men respond emotionally to their lovers' calls from outside a window and their relationships are cemented when one man comes to another through an open window; both novels have scenes in the British Museum and in both the lower-class men are saved at the last moment from emigrating to Buenos Aires or to Canada; both censure the restrictive sexual laws of England and argue for the freer laws of Sweden or of France; and in both the hero moves, as *The Longest Journey* states, 'from disgust to penitence, from penitence to longing, from a life of horror to a new life'. In the earlier novel Ansell 'had sheltered the fugitives [Rickie and Stephen] and given them money, and saved them from the ludicrous checks that so often stop young men';[35] and Maurice warns Alec: 'All the world's against us. We've got to pull ourselves together and make plans, while we can.'

Like *Maurice*, *The Longest Journey*, Forster's favourite and most autobiographical novel, was clearly written by a frail and unattractive intellectual who admired and craved the reality of the physical — from Gerald Dawes' muscles to the clayey soil of Wiltshire. The characters in *Maurice* were patterned too closely on those in *The Longest Journey*, so it is now clear that the lameness of the 'effeminate' Rickie (who hated his father and loved his mother, and 'can't ever marry owing to his foot') and the bastardy of Stephen ('He was illicit, abnormal, worse than a man diseased') are symbols of their homosexuality. The novel presents Forster's bitterest portrayal of a painfully unhappy marriage, and Rickie abandons Agnes (his first love failure) for Stephen ('dowered with coarse kindness and rustic strength') as Maurice leaves Clive for Alec.

In *The Longest Journey*, Rickie is first attracted to Agnes not when she intrudes on the all-male world of Cambridge, but when he has a 'vision' of her ('She was never to be so real to him again') embraced by Gerald Dawes, an athletic soldier who once bullied and degraded him at school. Though Rickie explicitly states that he can never replace Gerald, he marries the dominating and corrupting Agnes after Gerald's death, and returns to suffer in the public school milieu. Just before Rickie runs off with Stephen, both Agnes and Rickie notice and are attracted by Stephen's physical resemblance to Gerald. At the end of the novel Rickie 'saves' Stephen from a railway train but has his own legs cut off at the knees, like the Demeter of Cnidus whose picture adorns Stephen's room. This accident removes Rickie's abnormality (the lame foot) just before he dies, completes his symbolic castration by Agnes, and most importantly, severs the homosexual (and incestuous) relationship which Forster takes up again in *Maurice.*

The close similarities between *The Longest Journey* and *Maurice* suggest the imaginative limitations of the later novel, for the homosexual theme that is oblique, ambiguous and interesting in the earlier work becomes flat, banal and dull when it surfaces in *Maurice.* It is unsatisfactory as a homosexual novel because the stilted language and shrill emotions of the hero, a rather stiff prig out of Meredith, reveal virtually nothing about male love. In a Terminal Note Forster writes that the spark for *Maurice* was kindled on a 1913 visit to Edward Carpenter and his lover George Merrill, when the latter gently touched Forster's backside and the novelist rather fancifully imagined 'that at that precise moment I had conceived' (235). This self-conscious use of a gynecomorphous metaphor to describe the inspiration of the novel is characteristically false and coy.

Though Forster could not be frank about the pain of homosexual love, as Gide and Proust were, he could have learned from the superb example of *Death in Venice*, published in 1912 the year before he began *Maurice.* There is a paragraph in *Maurice* (and it is far too short) where the hero responds to a lascivious sign from an aged homosexual and then knocks him down, and he 'saw in this disgusting and dishonourable old age his own'. This is thematically similar to the scene when Aschenbach is revolted by an old invert on the boat to Venice, and ironically becomes very like him at the end of the novella. Unlike Forster, Mann portrays Aschenbach's yearning for Tadzio ambiguously and suggests that a homosexual love, though modelled on Hellenic idealism, is a degrading and destructive passion.

For Forster, it usually was destructive. The happy ending of *Maurice* was alien to his experience, for Maurice intends to live with

Alec 'outside class, without relations or money' and this is precisely what Forster (who lived with his mother until he was 66)[36] could never bring himself to do. *My Father and Myself* (1968), the brilliant posthumous autobiography of Forster's close friend, J. R. Ackerley (whom Forster introduced to a homosexual Hindu court in India) exposes the darker sides of inversion that are minimized in *Maurice.* Ackerley was unable to write for nearly fifteen years, and spent much of his free time hanging about places like the Piccadilly Station lavatory and hoping for a homosexual pick-up. Forster and Ackerley's frank and voluminous correspondence, now in the University of Texas Library, reveals that Forster also suffered and was often incapacitated by his hopeless love (or lust) for working-class youths, who drained off a good deal of his money.[37] (Like Maurice, he was unable to establish sexual relations with men of his own class.) His letters to Ackerley range from a witty note inviting his friend to tea with Forster's mother — providing he does not mention 'cockstands' — to a detailed description of Forster's sexual relations with a young man whose wife is in the same house. Like Rickie's mother in *The Longest Journey*, Forster sometimes had to go to Stockholm to find the sexual freedom denied him in England.

Maurice is essentially a study in repression and guilt — 'if you do a thing you're damned, and if you don't you're damned . . . [but] after all, is not a real Hell better than a manufactured Heaven?' — in which the hero manages to rid himself of both. Forster notes in his diary for 1911, the year after he published *Howards End*, 'a cause of my sterility is weariness of the only subject that I both can and may treat — the love of men for women & vice versa'.[38] Despite its lack of conviction, *Maurice* was a *therapeutic* success, for Forster had to exorcise the homosexual themes that moved so threateningly within his early works before he could complete his final masterpiece, *A Passage to India*, begun in 1912 but not finished until 1924. As George Steiner writes: 'The encounters between white and native, between emancipated rulers and 'advanced' Indians, in *A Passage to India*, are a brilliant projection of the confrontations between society and the homosexual in *Maurice*'.[39] 'Ecstasy cannot last', Forster writes in that novel, 'but can carve a channel for something lasting.' *Maurice*'s gentle satire, elegant style and certain thinness of substance suggest a line of English writers — William Plomer, Christopher Isherwood,

Angus Wilson — who have followed the Forsterian tradition in their fictional treatment of homosexuality.

III. THE LIFE TO COME

Despite Forster's didactic and sometimes facetious intent, the eight homosexual stories in *The Life to Come* (1972) are guilt-ridden and joyless episodes in which frightened, 'normal', upper-middle-class men — whose mistresses, wives and children fail to satisfy them — understand 'one another with a precision impossible for lovers' (103). These men overcome racial, social and sexual prejudices, and achieve temporary liberation by sodomizing an obliging and acquiescent farmer, milkman, Indian, soldier, sailor, policeman and even an animated statue, before lapsing back into their 'apparatus of decay' or plunging to a violent death.

Though the stories were written between 1922 and 1958 and the homosexual theme is overt, Forster's arch language and prudish heartiness — 'he gave the zip at the throat a downward pull. Much slid into view' (102) — firmly fix them in the Edwardian age. In 'The Other Boat' Forster writes: 'a muscle thickened up out of gold'. He seemed to think the penis was a muscle and was as naïve about anatomy as he was about the detrimental effects of masturbation. It is both surprising and depressing to discover that these puerile, pathetic, sentimental and thoroughly unimaginative fantasies, which lack Forster's characteristic subtlety and wit, actually excited the elderly novelist and occupied his creative mind for forty years. In 'The Obelisk', for example, an unattractive couple are temporarily revived when the wife is serviced by one sailor and the husband sodomized by another, after the crudely symbolic obelisk has 'fallen right over into the landslip upside-down, and the tip of it's gone in ever so far' (128).

The brief excerpts from Forster's diary and letters, quoted in the Introduction, are more interesting than the fictional leavings. When Forster completed *A Passage to India* in 1923 he told Siegfried Sassoon, 'I shall never write another novel after it — my patience with *ordinary* people has given out' (xiv). Unlike Proust, who transformed his 'secretary' Alberto into the fictional Albertine, Forster never wrote about homosexual love in a heterosexual disguise.

These posthumously published tales substantiate the criticism of Forster made by his contemporaries more than a half-century ago. Katherine Mansfield felt that Forster hints at passion in novels but does not examine it honestly and 'never gets any further than warming the teapot. He's a rare fine hand at that. Feel the teapot. Is it not beautifully warm? Yes, but there ain't going to be no tea.'[40] And Lytton Strachey recorded, after a house party in the 1920s: 'Morgan was charming at the week-end . . . He read two stories to C[arrington] and me — improper — quite amusing — but there always seems to be a trace of Weybridge in his style, whatever the subject may be.'[41] These stories were amusing precisely because they were improper, and in the days when inversion and pornography were illegal, these underground writings could only circulate privately among homosexual writers like Strachey, Sassoon[42] and T. E. Lawrence. But they nevertheless retained the stigma of suburban and bourgeois respectability which Strachey associated with Weybridge. Strachey defiantly pursued his passion with a bravado and panache that was totally lacking in the guarded Forster, whom Bloomsbury had nicknamed 'The Taupe'.

D. H. Lawrence, who was fond of diagnosing the sexual malaises of his friends and had tried to make Forster 'pregnant with his own soul', intuitively sensed the desperately unhappy repression and self-deception in Forster, who 'never had a sexual affair until he was in his forties'.[43] As Lawrence wrote in February 1915: 'Forster is here. He is very nice. I wonder if the grip has gone out of him. I get a feeling of acute misery from him — not that he does anything — but you know the acute, exquisite pain of cramp — I somehow feel that . . . He knows that self-realisation is not his ultimate desire.'[44]

When Forster finally discovered sex in the 1920s, his reaction was as banal and conventional as that of his liberated heroines who 'had lived and were saved': 'Her knees were trembling, her heart thumping' (122). Forster wrote to J. R. Ackerley in 1925 that his passion for Tom, a Weybridge bus driver, made him want to die because his ten minutes of previous happiness had been extended to nine hours and had been interrupted only because Tom's pregnant wife was about to give birth to their child. Two years later Forster revealed one of his fantasies to Ackerley during a discussion of the secretions of the sexual glands and wrote that he would like to retain his own testicles while adding a third that belong to someone else.[45]

Forster's fantasies, like his stories, continued into old age. In 1966-7, when Ackerley was in his sixties and Forster in his eighties, the former felt 'old, on the shelf, half deaf, written out, fucked out', and wrote that Morgan's 'sight may not be good, but it is *quite* good enough to see a male nude . . . [Morgan is] getting rather senile, poor darling. We drift apart a little, I fear. I hardly dare to look at a robin, he prefers to talk about human cockstands.'[46]

As Forster himself recognized, his stories of inversion were pornographic in intent and created as a kind of literary masturbation: 'These were written not to express myself but to excite myself' (xii). They are all rather precious, freighted with coincidence, and filled with fantasy and sudden violence; and the sexual scenes often take place in the symbolic unconscious — in a berth below deck or deep in a wood. The dominant theme is, once again, the 'call to life', where the vital impulse temporarily triumphs over safety and reason, and a miraculous transformation is achieved through a homosexual encounter: 'He looked handsomer than usual, and happier, and his lips were parted in a natural smile' (129). Forster writes in his diary of 1935, 'I want to love a strong young man of the lower classes and be loved by him and even hurt by him' (xiv), and in 'The Torque' and 'The Other Boat' there is a masochistic awareness and enjoyment of pain. In the former the discomfort of anal penetration by a Goth who is 'membered like horses' prevents Marcian from mounting his own horse; and in the latter Lionel March 'feared his own strength and was always gentle, and closed on him' (173). He then asks: ' "Did I hurt?" "Yes." "Sorry." "Why?" ' (178).

Forster's repressed hero is always condescending and patronizing, and the liaison with his inferior, no matter how successful, is quite deliberately ephemeral. In 'Arthur Snatchfold', 'The affair had been trivial and crude, and yet they both had behaved perfectly. They would never meet again, and they did not exchange names. After a hearty handshake, the young man swung away down the path, the sunlight and shadow rushing over his back' (104). Forster concedes that the affair was trivial and crude; and the inferior's behaviour is perfect because he knows his place, remains acquiescent, tactfully accepts payment and causes no trouble. The milkman is arrested in the sacred wood as soon as he walks off, and we are expected to believe that he willingly goes to prison to save an elderly gentleman whom he 'would never meet again'.

The two most ambitious stories, 'The Life to Come' and 'The Other Boat', are separated by forty years, have the same plot and repeat the climactic defenestration-suicide in 'The Story of a Panic'. In that early tale the priggish narrator remarks that 'this habit of promiscuous intimacy was perfectly intolerable, and could only lead to familiarity and mortification'; and the Italian satyr, Gennaro, who says that the Englishman 'longed for a friend, and found none for fifteen years. Then he found me', leaps to his death from a window.[47] Both posthumous stories concern the relations between an Englishman and his aromatic and sensual Indian lover, and both end in disaster. In the former the naked Indian stabs the Englishman to death and jumps off the roof, and in the latter the Englishman, 'with the seeds of love on him', stabs the naked Indian and jumps off the ship. In both stories stabbing is a symbolic destruction of the sexual instinct.

Two of the stories have a curious origin. In 'The Classical Annex', the Curator sees the fig leaves fall off a sculpture and observes 'an obscene change in the statue's physique'. After the Curator's premature retirement the museum acquires 'The Wrestling Lesson' and the working-class Town Councillor remarks: ' "Very nice piece, very decent. Look 'ow the elder brother's got the little chappie down. Look 'ow well the little chappie's taking it" ' (150).

This story was probably inspired by Vicenzo di Rossi's obscene statue of the muscular Hercules and Diomedes which stands in the Hall of the 500 in the Palazzo Vecchio in Florence. In his eighth labour Hercules struggled with and killed Diomedes, the King of Thrace who fed his mares human flesh. This statue shows Diomedes, held upside down with his legs open and sexual organs near Hercules' head, grasping Hercules' private parts. Forster sent Ackerley a postcard (now in Texas) of this popular cliché of pornographic sculpture with an appropriately witty allusion.

'The Torque' illustrates Lytton Strachey's witty retort when asked what he would do if a man tried to rape his sister: 'I would attempt to interpose myself between them'. For when Marcian and his holy sister Perpetua are attacked by savage Goths, 'Marcian intervened to save her . . . "I will hold them off for you. Escape." She escaped and he got raped' (158). Like the matches in 'The Obelisk' and the hairbrush in 'The Other Boat', the torque is a fetishistic symbol ('It had been round his lover's neck once. He swayed against

it and found himself in his lover's arms' (163)); and it is characteristic
of Forster that at this crucial moment of the story he lapses into
Virgilian tags: '*distillat ab inguine virus*' (the slimy fluid oozes from his
groin) — like the Life of Tiberius in an expurgated version.

Perhaps the most interesting story is 'Dr Woolacott', a kind of
Lady Chatterley's Lover in which Connie is omitted, the gamekeeper
ministers to the Master, and homosexuality is treated as an illness
that can be 'cured' by an indulgent inoculation. In a moment of
critical aberration T. E. Lawrence, who was the model for the
'war-obsessed' stranger who liberates the invalid from death-in-life
to an exultant *Liebestod,* praised the story in a military-sexual
metaphor: 'The most powerful thing I ever read . . . more charged
with the real high explosive than anything I've ever met' (xiii).

Forster dedicated *The Eternal Moment* (1927) 'To T. E. in the
absence of anything else', and 'The Point of It' (1911) is the story in
that volume which Forster told Lawrence is 'a feeble timid
premonition of the [unpublishable] one which is with you now and
which is yours really, and that is what the dedication really means'.[48]
Forster wrote that his Bloomsbury friends did not like the grim yet
vague and elusive 'The Point of It', and when they queried: 'What *is*
the point?' he did not know what to reply. This early story portrays
two modes of life, that of Harold (Lawrence) — brief, violent,
fulfilled, and that of Micky (Forster) — respectable, though
somewhat dull and empty.

'Dr Woolacott' is more feeble though less timid than its feeble
timid premonition 'The Point of It'. Like the earlier story, 'Dr
Woolacott' describes the brief conjunction of contrasting characters.
Forster is Clesant, the weak son of a dead father, a chronic invalid
with a functional illness, surrounded in his country estate with
medicine bottles and air cushions, and sick 'of being myself'.
Lawrence is the *déclassé* labourer on his farm, recently recovered
from a serious head-wound which made his brains stick out like 'a
butcher's shop' but now, with broad shoulders and sunburnt throat,
'fresh as a daisy, strong as a horse', and determined to get the most
out of life. Clesant is slowly sinking under the ineffectual treatment
of Dr Woolacott. Though the severely repressed Clesant did not
think he could provoke desire, he imagined that 'They touched, their
limbs entwined, they gripped and grew mad with delight' (95).
Though this passionate dream seems to liberate the invalid, Dr

Woolacott arrives too late and finds his patient dead on the floor.

This weak story reveals more about Forster and Forster's view of Lawrence than about Lawrence himself. Like D. H. Lawrence in 1915, T. E. probably gave Forster some sound sexual advice which, as the minatory conclusion suggests, he was unable to follow. It is ironic that Forster portrayed Lawrence as an affirmer of life and was deceived by the apparent health and vitality that disguised his sexual pathology. Though Forster was more conventional, fearful and repressed, Lawrence's homosexuality was more self-destructive, and could be satisfied only by the whippings that punished the guilt of his submission at Deraa, tested the body and defiantly reaffirmed the power of the will.

Though Forster believed he would have been a more famous writer if he had published more of his fiction, neither *Maurice* nor the stories in *The Life to Come*, none of which is as good as 'The Road from Colonus' or 'The Eternal Moment', adds to his stature as an author. His editor, Oliver Stallybrass, is quite mistaken when he boasts that the two most ambitious tales 'show Forster at the height of his powers, with a tragic grandeur unequalled in his stories, and unsurpassed even in *A Passage to India*' (xvi). Despite Forster's promise in 'The Other Boat', the moment of ecstasy does not lead to the 'moment of vision' but merely to a kind of 'friendly curiosity'.

The homosexual stories in *The Life to Come* were better as therapy than as art. Though Forster writes in his Ruritanian fantasy, 'What Does It Matter?', 'Poking doesn't count . . . Try to imagine the old days when that sort of thing mattered, and emerge laughing' (140, 145), sex mattered a great deal to him and he could not laugh it away. His radically defective stories seem rather trivial and even indecent when compared to *The Immoralist, Death in Venice* and *Cities of the Plain*, where the homosexual theme transcends the purely personal and is transfigured into a literary masterpiece.

VIII

T. E. LAWRENCE
Seven Pillars of Wisdom

How can he be clean that is born of woman?
                                                        Job

That is the flesh, that is what I hate, and what makes me wish to die.
                                                General Charles Gordon

Seven Pillars of Wisdom (1926) is the story of Lawrence's growth in personal and political awareness. The meaning of the book is determined by the juxtaposition of his psychological needs and the pattern of historical events, by the conflict between the man who acts and the conditions of his action. Lawrence's role in the Arab Revolt combined self-discipline with freedom and power, and his devotion to the higher cause of a 'holy war' enabled him to define his identity. But for Lawrence this self-discovery was destructive rather than enlightening. He gradually realized that he had been transformed from a man who had once valued each human life and had given himself in the service of freedom, to one who had been caught up in a repellent and fascinating slaughter and had lost his idealism. When he was tortured and raped at Deraa, this insight deepened into the horrible realization that he had achieved sexual pleasure from physical pain.

The Deraa experience completely destroyed his elaborately constructed network of defences and exposed his all-too-human vulnerability, broke his spirit and extinguished the possibilities of creative freedom. This crucial moment — what Erik Erikson calls 'The Event', or culmination and turning point of a man's experience — dramatizes the central opposition of body and will, and forms the core of *Seven Pillars* as well as of Lawrence's life.

Lawrence's post-war career — his political activities, the composition of *Seven Pillars*, the enlistment in the ranks, the flagellations and even the suicidal motorcycle rides — followed inevitably from the events described in the book. For just as the idealism and repression of his early life seemed to prepare for and lead up to his crisis in Arabia, so everything that happened after it seemed to be a direct result of those two years, 1916-18, that synthesized the experience of a lifetime.

Nietzsche's concept of the will to power provided a philosophical foundation for Lawrence's idealistic ambitions, and the expression of the will through action was his means to self-knowledge. The supremacy of the will is affirmed by the force of its opposition, for as Nietzsche states: 'The will to power can manifest itself only against resistances; therefore it seeks that which resists it . . . It is *not* the satisfaction of the will that causes pleasure . . . but rather the will's forward thrust and again and again becoming master over that which stands in its way.'[1]

Nietzsche's theory that the will to power could dominate corporal needs and be employed as a creative force, not only gave Lawrence ideological support for his leadership of the Arab Revolt but also reinforced his hatred of the body. In a late chapter of *Seven Pillars* on the Turkish hospital, he writes of the 'slow physical corruption, a piecemeal rotting of the envelope of flesh about the hopeless spirit longing to escape'.[2] And in his play *Soldiers*, Rolf Hochhuth quotes Lawrence's statement that 'We racked ourselves with inherited remorse for the flesh-indulgence of our gross birth, striving to pay for it through a lifetime of misery'.[3] Much of Lawrence's life was an unsuccessful attempt to subjugate his body, and he tried to escape the humiliation of the physical ('Everything bodily is now hateful to me') through starvation, asceticism, masochism and even flagellation. To test and prove his will he would sometimes resort to trials of physical endurance, a degradation of the body that threw the mind into greater relief. St John Philby reports that on a freezing train ride through Jordan in 1921, 'we travelled ourselves on the engine, cowering as near the boiler as possible against the icy wind and driving sleet. Lawrence stood out on the dashboard the whole journey of three or four hours'.[4]

Lawrence's revulsion in the Tank Corps from the raw, lecherous carnality and the 'animal reek here which keeps me awake at night with the horror that mankind should be like it',[5] is very similar to Gulliver's horror and astonishment when he observes in the abominable Yahoo a disturbing likeness to himself. Leonard

Woolley relates that in Syria Lawrence 'came to a village where a number of Kurdish girls were drawing water from the well, and asked for a drink . . . One bold hussy pulled open his shirt to see if his skin was white all over; and soon, with shrieks of laughter, they were all about him determined to see more, until he escaped almost stripped. He could not take it as a joke.'[6] Lawrence's sexual shock is remarkably like Gulliver's after he is attacked when bathing by a female Yahoo: 'now I could no longer deny that I was a real Yahoo, in every Limb and Feature, since the Females had a natural Propensity to me as one of their own Species.'[7]

The bitter and enigmatic personality of Jonathan Swift provides a suggestive analogy to the divided Lawrence. Swift, a posthumous child and Lawrence, an illegitimate one, had radically disturbed and covertly hostile relationships with their parents. Each had a proud and anguished character, a horror of the physical side of life, a compulsive cleanliness, a perverse sexual attitude; and they also had a considerable achievement in both literature and politics, a number of brilliant and powerful friends, a soaring ambition briefly gratified and then permanently disappointed. The last part of their lives was spent in obscurity, amidst humble and adoring mediocrities.

Lawrence's mother was the dominant influence in his life. She too was an illegitimate child, brought up under the rigorous regimen of Presbyterian puritanism, which she powerfully impressed on her son. She was sent to Ireland as a young woman to be a maid in the house of Sir Thomas Chapman, Lawrence's father, who had long been married to an unstable, unattractive and unsympathetic woman. Though passion momentarily overcame repression when she ran off with Sir Thomas (who could never obtain a divorce), she soon reverted to an even more fanatical religion as the 'sinful' birth of her five sons repeated her mother's 'crime' and intensified her own fears of damnation. Lawrence's father died during the influenza epidemic of 1919; and in 1922, when she was 61 years old, the strong-willed Sarah Lawrence continued her penance, joined her eldest son Bob, and became a missionary in China. She died in 1959 at the age of 98.

The origins of Lawrence's sexual pathology can be clarified by Shakespeare's *Hamlet*, for both Hamlet and Lawrence react to the guilt-ridden, irregular marriage of their mothers, to whom they are unusually close, with a violent sexual revulsion. Hamlet's nauseated condemnation of living

> In the rank sweat of an enseamèd bed,
> Stewed in corruption, honeying and making love
> Over the nasty sty (III.iv.92-4)

is an accurate portrayal of Lawrence's sexual morbidity and of the impossibility of escaping the 'corruption of lust'. As D. H. Lawrence writes of the tortured Prince: 'A sense of corruption in the flesh makes Hamlet frenzied, for he will never admit that it is his own flesh'.[8]

Undoubtedly disturbed by his parents' sexual relationship, Lawrence adopted David Hogarth as a 'purer' surrogate father[9] and Charlotte Shaw as his substitute mother. Lawrence felt he could confide in the older married woman (he believed women are unfortunate when they have sexual relations with men)[10] and Mrs Shaw was 65 when she first met Lawrence in 1922, the year his mother left for China. Charlotte Shaw, who shared Lawrence's idea of 'sexlessness' and inviolate virginity, never slept with her husband, Bernard Shaw. Lawrence established a surprising intimacy with her, adopted her name in 1925, and made some extraordinary revelations about his family and himself in his letters to her.

> My mother [was] brought up as a child of sin in the Island of Skye by a bible-thinking Presbyterian, then a nurse-maid, then 'guilty' (in her judgement) of taking my father from his wife [and four daughters] . . . My father was on the large scale, tolerant, experienced, grand, rash, humoursome . . . a spendthrift, a sportsman, and a hard rider and drinker . . . She was wholly wrapped up in my father . . . whom she kept as her trophy of power. Also she was a fanatical housewife . . . To justify herself, she remodelled my father, making him a teetotaler . . . They thought always that they were living in sin, and that we would someday find it out. Whereas I knew it before I was ten, and they never told me; till after my father's death something I said showed mother that I knew, and didn't care a straw . . . I have a terror of her knowing anything about my feelings, or convictions, or way of life. If she knew they would be damaged: violated: no longer mine. You see, she would not hesitate to understand them: and I

do not understand them, and do not want to . . . Knowledge of her will prevent my ever making any woman a mother, and the cause of children. I think she suspects this . . . They should not have borne children.[11]

This remarkable letter from the normally reticent Lawrence reveals a number of crucial points. It is clear that the withdrawn and ascetic Lawrence inherited few of his father's grand and magnificent characteristics and a great many of his mother's. After considerable conflict, the mother totally dominated and completely transformed the father, who was not merely a drinker but a hopeless drunkard,[12] and her sons too became trophies of her authoritarian power. Her fanaticism manifested itself not only in religion but also in the extremes of cleanliness and discipline, and she often usurped the father's role and punished her sons with humiliating whippings on their bare bodies.[13] Lawrence tried to escape from his parents' discord by moving to a small cottage in the garden, and he joined the artillery in 1906 because of trouble at home and 'did eight months before being bought out'.[14] Lawrence grew up in an atmosphere of overwhelming sin and guilt, and discovered the source of this guilt just as he was entering the vulnerable period of adolescence. His statement that he 'didn't care a straw' is a rather unconvincing whistling in the dark. It is difficult to assess (but easy to underestimate) the influence of Lawrence's illegitimacy on his personality, but it must have intensified, if not determined, his odd combination of shy reserve and provocative aggressiveness, his intense alienation and isolation, and his sense of shame and degradation. (He could have been the recognized son of a baronet, and he was never acknowledged by his father's family even after his achievements had made him famous. This sensitivity about the stigma of illegitimacy is portrayed in Conrad's *Under Western Eyes* where Razumov, the son of the aloof Prince Kirylo, 'was as lonely in the world as a man swimming in the deep sea'.[15])

The letter to Charlotte Shaw also shows that Lawrence felt his mother threateningly close to him, and because she was able to pierce the core of his inner self, he had to erect a barrier of secrecy to protect himself from her.[16] (The lengthy descriptions of castles in the *Home Letters* are an attempt to maintain a formal distance from his mother.) Because of their strong similarity, Lawrence developed a keen insight into his mother's puritanical shame and guilt. This perception did not liberate him from his mother's feelings, but led to a revulsion and disgust that prevented him from ever having sexual relations with women. He proudly proclaims his virginity and rejects the dirty feeling of sex in an unpublished letter to Robert Graves;[17] and in another letter to Charlotte Shaw, speaks of a woman's unbearable humiliation in sexual union.[18] In *Seven Pillars* Lawrence's response to the realities of heterosexual relations was either a naïve and unconvincing dismissal of the unhygienic pleasure of our comic reproductive processes (356), or a horrified revulsion: 'I asked how they could look with pleasure on children, embodied proof of their consummated lust?'[19] (508). He admired the Greek epitaph: 'Here I lie of Tarsus / Never having married, and would that my father had not.'

One of the ways that Lawrence came to terms with his body was through a kind of Greek idealization (inspired by Achilles and Patroclus) of male love. This homosexual union in an exclusively masculine society, represented in *Seven Pillars* by the love of Farraj and Daud, Lawrence considered more honest, innocent and spiritual than heterosexual love. Mrs Lawrence, in a deceptively wholesome statement, told Robert Graves, 'We could never be bothered with girls in our house';[20] and for Lawrence, the Arab Revolt was a recreation of this domestic atmosphere, for 'there was nothing female in the Arab movement, but the camels' (221). In an essay on *Arabia Deserta*, the homosexual novelist, Norman Douglas, coyly writes: 'We could have been given glimpses into certain secret things, certain customs of profound significance in Oriental life and of interest to the European students. Doughty, with a kind of maidenly modesty, barely hints at their existence.'[21] Lawrence amply provides what Doughty omits, and portrays the permissive atmosphere of Arabic male love, first made notorious in Gide's *The Immoralist*, where young Arab boys reveal their golden nudity beneath soft, flowing robes.

Male passion had to be satisfied in the desert, sometimes through bestiality with the flocks of sheep or with the raddled meat of prostitutes. In the very first chapter Lawrence challenges conventional morality and writes that 'friends quivering together in the yielding sand with intimate hot limbs in supreme embrace, found there hidden in the darkness a sensual co-efficient of the mental passion which was welding our souls and spirits into one flaming effort' (28). For Lawrence, the clean, indifferent male bodies are not only a comparatively pure alternative to venereal disease, but also have the advantage of providing political as well as sexual unity. Lawrence's desire for 'these partnerships of man and man, to supply human nature with more than the contact of flesh with flesh' (521), was realized not only in his writing but also in his life, where there is continual evidence of homosexuality, especially in his relations with Sheik Ahmed, to whom he dedicated *Seven Pillars*.

Sheik Ahmed or Dahoum (he was known by both names), of mixed Arab and Hittite blood, was 14 when the 23-year-old Lawrence met him with the other workers at the Carchemish archeological site in 1911. Leonard Woolley, Lawrence's colleague and co-author, reproduces some photographs of the lovely but 'not particularly intelligent' boy in *Dead Towns and Living Men*, and gives the most complete picture of him. Dahoum was

> beautifully built and remarkably handsome. Lawrence was devoted to him. The Arabs were tolerantly scandalized by the friendship, especially when in 1913 Lawrence, stopping in the house after the dig was over, had Dahoum to live with him and got him to pose as a model for a queer crouching figure which he carved in the soft local limestone and set up on the edge of the house roof; to make an image was bad enough in its way, but to portray a naked figure was proof to them of evil of another sort. The scandal about Lawrence was widely spread and firmly believed . . . He knew quite well what the Arabs said about himself and Dahoum and so far from resenting it was amused, and I think he courted misunderstanding rather than tried to avoid it.[22]

Lawrence formed a blood-brotherhood with Dahoum, and in 1912 writes enthusiastically to his parents that 'Dahoum is very useful now, though a savage: however we are here in the feudal system, which gives the overlord great claims: so that I have no trouble with him: he wrestles beautifully, better than all of his age & size'.[23] Lawrence took Dahoum to England in 1913 and to Sinai in 1914, when he and Woolley mapped the wilderness of Zin. Dahoum died of typhus behind Turkish lines in 1918, and it is conceivable that one of Lawrence's motives for the secret reconnaissance behind enemy

lines to Baalbek and Damascus in May-June 1917 was to see
Dahoum: 'I drew these tides of men into my hands/. . . that your
eyes might be shining for me/When we came'.[24]

Lawrence also attracted a number of sensitive, intelligent and
creative men (as well as elderly maternal women), and had
extremely close friendships with Vyvyan Richards and Ernest
Altounyan (both of whom have suggested they were in love with
Lawrence); with the homosexual writers James Hanley, Frederic
Manning and E. M. Forster; and with young airmen like the
beautiful, blond and blue-eyed R. A. Guy (whom he called 'Rabbit'
or 'Poppet') and to whom he writes: 'My pleasure in the R.A.F. was
partly, largely, due to the pleasure I got from your blue and yellow
self: I owe you a deep debt for many happy times.'[25]

A second letter to Charlotte Shaw, written a year later, revives the
earlier themes of his mother's dominance, his frightening similarity
to her, his ambivalent attraction-repulsion, her probing search into
his privacy, her vicarious existence in her children's lives, and her
insatiable demand for love, especially after the death of two sons in
the war.

> She is monumental really: and so unlike you. Probably she is
> exactly like me: otherwise we wouldn't so hanker after one
> another, whenever we are wise enough to keep apart. Her letters
> are things I dread, and she always asks for more of mine (I try to
> write monthly: but we haven't a subject we dare to be intimate
> upon: so they are spavined things) and hates them when they
> come, as they do, ever so rarely. I think I'm afraid of letting her
> get, ever so little, inside the circle of my integrity: and she is
> always hammering and sapping to come in. A very dominant
> person: only old now, and, so my brother says, very much less
> than she had been. She has lived so in her children, & in my father,
> that she cannot relieve herself, upon herself, and from herself, at
> all. And it isn't right to cry out to your children for love. They are
> prevented by the walls of time and function, from loving their
> parents.[26]

Lawrence's language in these two letters is strikingly close to his
description of his torture and rape at Deraa. His mother's 'sapping' is
a metaphor of siege and assault, and also has the suggestion of sexual
debilitation. Lawrence's terror that 'if she knew [his feelings] they

would be damaged: *violated*: no longer mine' and his fear 'of letting her get . . . inside the circle of my *integrity*' is emotionally and psychologically connected to the last sentence of the Deraa chapter: 'the passing days confirmed how in Deraa that night the citadel of my integrity had been irrevocably lost'. The greatest childhood fear of his mother was realized in the most horrible and degrading moment of Lawrence's life.

Though Lawrence was often the only witness to the events he records, and his veracity has been questioned, most notably by Richard Aldington, the memoirs of his comrades and enemies confirm the essential accuracy of his account of the Arab Revolt. Similarly, the longer Oxford edition of *Seven Pillars* and Lawrence's extremely frank letters to Charlotte Shaw give the complete revelation of what is portrayed only indirectly in the published version of his book.

Like Proust, Lawrence subjects this experience to a minute and introspective analysis, as if he wanted his mind to be an objective observer of his flesh's suffering in order to understand it and make it bearable. But this event was extremely difficult for him to record; and even Lawrence, with his capacity for Proustian self-revelation, was unable to write the distinct truth and was forced to portray it obliquely. As he says in a moving letter to Edward Garnett:

> If that Deraa incident whose treatment you call severe and serene (the second sounds like a quaint failure to get my impressions across, but I know what you feel) had happened to yourself you would not have recorded it. I have a face of brass perhaps, but I put it into print very reluctantly, last of all the pages I sent to the press. For weeks I wanted to burn it in the manuscript: because I could not tell the story face to face with anyone, and I think I'll feel sorry, when I next meet you, that you know it. The sort of man I have always mixed with doesn't so give himself away.[27]

Chapter 80 on Deraa, in which Lawrence discusses his greatest personal failure, appears within the context of Book 6, which narrates his greatest military failure: his inability to destroy the railway bridges in the Yarmuk Valley. And Chapter 80, the antithesis of his triumphs at Aqaba, Jerusalem and Damascus, is closely related to the avenging massacre of the Deraa police battalion in the battle of Tafas, where Lawrence ordered that no prisoners be taken.

In this chapter, Lawrence describes his torture with a nearly intolerable precision that has become a model for the torture scenes in books like *Days of Wrath* and *1984.* Disguised as a Circassian, Lawrence is captured on a reconnaissance behind enemy lines, and after violently rejecting the depraved assault of a Turkish Bey, he is tortured into submission. A soldier

> began to lash me madly across and across with all his might, while I locked my teeth to endure this thing which lapped itself like a flaming wire about my body . . . [I] could feel only the shapeless weight of pain, not tearing claws, for which I had prepared, but a gradual cracking apart of my whole being by some too-great force whose waves rolled up my spine till they were pent within my brain, to clash terribly together . . . [The men] would squabble for the next turn, ease themselves, and play unspeakably with me . . . A hard white ridge, like a railway, darkening slowly into crimson, leaped over my skin at the instant of each stroke, with a bead of blood where two ridges crossed. As the punishment proceeded the whip fell more and more upon existing weals, biting blacker or more wet, till my flesh quivered with accumulated pain, and with terror of the next blow coming . . . At last when I was completely broken they seemed satisfied (453-4).

The sadistic ingenuity of the depraved torturers is as fearful as humiliation, suffering or death; and this extreme moment represents the ultimate punishment for the accumulated fear and guilt — personal, political and military — of a lifetime. As in Kafka's Penal Colony, the crime is literally imprinted on the body of the victim. The fissured waves of spinal pain recall the 'waves of feeling' evoked in the first chapter and the 'waves that had been dashing themselves against the coasts of flesh' in the third, and synthesize Lawrence's intense guilt about his supposed betrayal of the Arab Revolt. The 'flaming wire' and 'railway darkening into crimson' reflect not only his unsuccessful detonations but also his guilt about the innocent civilians who had been killed by his successful railway explosions. The homosexual rape ('ease themselves') leads to the terrifying realization that a part of him wants to be sodomized.

In *Seven Pillars* Lawrence is taken to the Turkish Bey who 'rejected me in haste, as a thing too torn and bloody for his bed' (454), and who instead of Lawrence takes a Turkish soldier for his pleasure. But in an agonizing letter to Charlotte Shaw, Lawrence admits the truth: that he lost his nerve and sexually surrendered when he could no longer bear the pain.

> You instance my night in Deraa. Well, I'm always afraid of being hurt: and to me, while I live, the force of that night will lie in the agony which broke me, and made me surrender . . . For fear of being hurt, or rather to earn five minutes respite from a pain which drove me mad, I gave away the only possession we are born into the world with — our bodily integrity. It's an unforgivable matter, an irrevocable position: and it's that which has made me forswear decent living, and the exercise of my not-contemptible wits and talents.
>
> You may call this morbid: but think of the offence, and the intensity of my brooding over it for these years. It will hang about me while I live, and afterwards if our personality survives. Consider wandering among the decent ghosts, hereafter, crying 'unclean, unclean!'[28]

The phrase, 'will hang about me', is an allusion to the albatross in 'The Ancient Mariner', and the final words refer to the pariah-leper in Leviticus 13:45 who rends his clothes, bares his head, covers his lips, and cries 'unclean, unclean' through the deserted streets. Like the leper, Lawrence feels he is to blame for his uncleanness.

Lawrence told Graves that he suffers 'a loss of integrity'[29] when physically touched, and his strong sense of protective purity and cleanness, his virginal ideal of *'Noli me tangere'*, is vitally connected to his definition of himself. In the midst of this torture, the ambiguous algolagnia and homosexuality of the illegitimate, celibate[30] and ascetic Lawrence, are suddenly revealed: 'I remembered the corporal kicking with his nailed boot . . . [and] remembered smiling idly at him, for a delicious warmth, probably sexual, was swelling through me' (454).[31] In this terrifying epiphany, Lawrence overcomes his obsessive childhood fear of pain and becomes like the Arabs, for whom pain was 'a solvent, a cathartic, almost a decoration, to be fairly worn while they survived

it' (476). But the punishment for this perverse pleasure is instan-
taneous:

> He flung up his arm and hacked with the full length of his whip
> into my groin. This doubled me half-over, screaming, or rather,
> trying impotently to scream, only shuddering through my open
> mouth . . . Another slash followed. A roaring, and my eyes went
> black: while within me the core of life seemed to heave slowly up
> through the rending nerves, expelled from its body by this last
> indescribable pang. (454)

During the preliminary perversions, Lawrence had kicked the Bey
in the testicles, and it seems clear from this passage that 'the core of
life' which heaves up slowly like an orgasm, is Lawrence's oblique
metaphorical revelation that the unbearable pain in his sexual organs
forced him to give in to the rape. The lost citadel of his integrity (in
its root meaning: soundness, health, purity and honesty) is his
spiritual destruction.

The Oxford version of this chapter concludes with a long,
sensitive, poignant passage, omitted from the final text, in which
Lawrence probes deeper into his seared psyche than perhaps
anywhere else in the entire book and clarifies that longing for
self-immolation that would not leave him for the rest of his life:

> I was feeling very ill, as though some part of me had gone dead
> that night in Deraa, leaving me maimed, imperfect, only half
> myself. It could not have been the defilement, for no one ever held
> the body in less honour than I did myself. Probably it had been the
> breaking of the spirit by that frenzied nerve-shattering pain which
> had degraded me to the beast level when it made me grovel to it,
> and which had journeyed with me since, a fascination and terror
> and morbid desire, lascivious and vicious, perhaps, but like the
> striving of a moth towards its flame.[32]

This torture broke the violent trajectory of Lawrence's life and
taught him that the spirit is ultimately dependent on the 'beast level'
of the body. He comments profoundly on this episode, which he
understood but could not accept, when he relates how

> The practice of our revolt fortified the nihilist attitude in me.
> During it, we often saw men push themselves or be driven to a

cruel extreme of endurance: yet never was there an intimation of physical break. Collapse rose always from a moral weakness eating into the body, which of itself, without traitors from within, had no power over the will. (477)

Lawrence had sought to make himself pure will, independent of his body. But when he discovered his perverse sexuality, the 'traitor within', his will broke and 'the citadel of his integrity' was irrevocably lost.

After Deraa, Lawrence's will could no longer drive his body and his asceticism degenerated to a wish for annihilation:

I was tired to death of free-will, and of many things besides free-will. For a year and a half I had been in motion, riding a thousand miles each month upon camels: with added nervous hours in crazy aeroplanes, or rushing across country in powerful cars. In my last five actions I had been hit, and my body so dreaded further pain that now I had to force myself under fire. Generally I had been hungry: lately always cold: and frost and dirt had poisoned my hurts into a festering mass of sores.

However, these worries would have taken their due petty place, in my despite of the body, and of my soiled body in particular, but for the rankling fraudulence which had to be my mind's habit . . . My will had gone and I feared to be alone, lest the winds of circumstance, or power, or lust, blow my empty soul away. (514)

This is the tragic mood with which the book ends: the ultimate wisdom of his empty triumph is the clean escape of death, man's 'last free will, a saving grace and measure of intolerable pain'.

In passages from the Oxford text, omitted from the final edition, Lawrence shudders at 'the almost insane tension of too-constant striving after an ideal', and confesses that 'my will, the worn instrument which had so long frayed our path, broke suddenly in my hand and fell useless. It told me that this Eastern chapter in my life was ended'.[33]

In *White Jacket*, a novel that Lawrence read and admired, Melville describes two possible reactions to flogging. In some men, the 'feeling of the innate dignity remaining untouched, though outwardly the body be scarred for the whole term of the natural life, is one of the hushed things, buried among the holiest privacies of the soul'; but the weaker and less fortunate victim, like Lawrence, 'is never the man he was before, but, broken and shattered to the marrow of his bones, sinks into death before his time'.[34] Jock Chambers, a close friend of Lawrence during his years in the R.A.F., has told me that Lawrence was completely shattered when he enlisted, and writes that, 'When asleep he continually repeated a horrible experience of his war-time days'.[35]

Lawrence's sexual surrender at Deraa and his homosexuality that was so inextricably a part of it led to a desire for self-punishment and humiliation. After the war he became an 'extinct volcano' and, like Conrad's Razumov and Lord Jim, experienced a moral self-betrayal and dishonourable fall from self-esteem that intensified his guilt. Lawrence told Lionel Curtis that his masochism remains and will remain, and emphasizes that self-degradation is his aim. 'I long for people to look down on me and despise me', he writes to Charlotte Shaw, 'and I'm too shy to take the filthy steps which would publicly shame me, and put me in their contempt'.[36]

This intense desire for self-degradation manifested itself in two significant ways. First, Lawrence abandoned the unlimited possibilities of a career in public life and voluntarily returned to his mother's class (the class that 'gave themselves away') in the 'lay monasticism' of the masculine military ranks: 'I'm afraid (physically afraid) of other men: their animal spirits seem to me the most terrible companions to haunt a man . . . What is it that makes me so damnably sensitive and so ready to cry out, and yet so ready to incur more pain?'[37] Secondly, while serving in the Tank Corps in 1923, Lawrence persuaded a young Scotsman, John Bruce, to flog him at regular intervals, which sometimes occurred on the anniversary of the Deraa torture and extended over a period of eleven years. Freud writes that 'Masochism includes a sense of guilt, which surges toward "redemption"'.[38] Though this ritualistic flagellation revived the sexual pleasure as well as the sexual guilt of Deraa, it obviously did not bring the redemption that the medieval flagellants hoped to achieve. To appreciate the true horror of these floggings, which are impossible to imagine fully, one should recall Proust's betrayal of a similar scene in *Time Regained*: the ruthless self-induced whipping of the Baron Charlus in the male brothel of Jupien.[39]

Though the precise reasons for Lawrence's scourging are complex and obscure, it is likely that the series of beatings exemplify the 'repetition-compulsion' which Freud discusses in *Beyond the Pleasure Principle* (1920) and relates to the death-instinct. The whippings are a re-enactment of Lawrence's terrible traumatic guilt, and allow him to redeem his eternal and existential debt by enduring what had once crushed his body and spirit, and to displace the death-instinct with self-punishment instead of self-destruction.

The desire for death is a powerful theme in *Seven Pillars* ('instinct said die'): in the opening lines to S.A. ('Death seemed my servant on the road . . .'), in his weary longing to be among the quiet and strangely beautiful corpses that he carefully arranges, and in his desire, after the destruction of his will, to have the winds blow his empty soul away. The death wish could be displaced but never eliminated, and was embodied in the frenetic speed passages in 'The Road' section of the masochistic *Mint* and finally realized in the pointless and fatal motorcycle accident.

Lawrence's death wish is significantly related to his passion for personal cleanliness and to his love of baths (his one sensual indulgence) as well as to the important theme of cleanness in *Seven Pillars*. Lawrence often describes the desert as clean ('the desert landscape cleansed me'), and it is a strong contrast to the 'filth' (blood, vomit and sperm) that is wiped off Lawrence as he lies 'retching and sobbing for mercy' after his flogging. In the last chapter of *Seven Pillars* Lawrence, on the verge of a nervous breakdown after the ultimate horrors of the Turkish hospital, laughs hysterically at an Australian major who then smacks him in the face. This symbolic slap recalls the slap of the Bey's bedroom slipper across his face before the torture at Deraa, and from this moment Lawrence becomes 'so stained in estimation that afterward nothing in the world would make him feel clean' (682). Only death 'would be a clean escape'. The epigraph stamped on the cover of the book — 'the sword also means clean-ness and death' — reinforces Lawrence's connection of cleanness with death, rather than with life. He specifically associates birth with uncleanness and filth, and invites the astonished Arabs to imagine the birth of children, who 'crawl worm-like out of the mother [a] bloody, blinded thing' (508). The core of Lawrence's, and Swift's, sexual pathology is their inability to accept the natural life-processes of birth and sex which are inevitably linked with women, and the terrible paradox that man is born between urine and feces, that 'Love has pitched his mansion in/The place of excrement'.

Lawrence's inability to accept this physiological fact is a cause of his hatred of the body, masochism, fear of his mother, revulsion from heterosexual love and homosexuality. All these are synthesized in one of his strangest and most revealing descriptions: an 'excremental vision' of a clogged women's toilet on the troop ship to India that has 'the horror of almost final squalidity' and exhibits the same inverted idealism as Swift's 'The Lady's Dressing Room'. The sergeant

> strides boldly to the latrine: 'Excuse me' unshyly to two shrinking women. 'God,' he jerked out, 'flooded with shit — where's the trap?' . . . The ordure rippled over his boots. Up his right sleeve, baring a forearm hairy as a mastiff's grey leg, knotted with veins, and a gnarled hand: thrust it deep in, groped, pulled out a moist white bundle. 'Open that port' and out it splashed into the night. 'You'd think they'd have had some other place for their sanitary towels. Bloody awful show.'[40]

'Bloody' is both literal and metaphorical, though Lawrence feels it is not 'human to go very far into the mechanism of life'.[41] The disgust and revulsion of this passage express Lawrence's extreme Swiftian misanthropy — 'had the world been mine I'd have left out animal life upon it'[42] — that leads directly and inevitably to a Nietzschean elimination of ordinary, unclean, birthing human beings: 'What is wanted is a new master species — birth control for us, to end the human race in fifty years — and then a clear field for some *cleaner* mammal. I suppose it must be a mammal.'[43]

In *Seven Pillars of Wisdom* inversion is dichotomized either as 'carnal marriage complemented by spiritual union'[44] among the Arabs or sickening sodomy among the Turks. But in Lawrence's case, homosexuality is the manifestation of the body's weakness in relation to the will. Lawrence hated his body's vulnerability and feared his barely repressed desires; and by disciplining and subjecting his corporal self he was able to channel his libido into war, achieve the outstanding feats of physical endurance and earn the respect of the Bedouin, which was vital to his leadership. But the assault by the despised Turkish enemy on his point of greatest weakness, his sexual core, subverted his will and powers of endurance, betrayed the high ideals of the dedicatory poem to S.A. ('the inviolate house as a memory to you'), ravished his bodily integrity and precious virginity, and set him on the path of renunciation and destruction.

D. H. LAWRENCE

The White Peacock, Women in Love, Aaron's Rod, The Plumed Serpent

Every man comprises male and female in his being, the male always struggling for predominance.

Study of Thomas Hardy

D. H. Lawrence believed his intrinsic sexual nature was dual and not entirely male, and that his male and female elements were in conflict, not in balance. This mixture gave him great insight into the female being, a considerable advantage to a creative writer. But it also caused him to see sexual relationships in terms of struggle rather than harmony, and led to a fear of merging rather than a confidence in union. Lawrence's novels describe a number of cruel and mutually destructive conflicts between men and women, as well as an alternative search for satisfying relationships between men.

Lawrence's conflicting attitudes about the possibility of male love are expressed throughout his works, where his life erupts into art, and most specifically in four overt homosexual scenes: the swimming idyll in *The White Peacock* (1911), the wrestling match in *Women in Love* (1920), the nursing episode in *Aaron's Rod* (1922) and the initiation ceremony in *The Plumed Serpent* (1926). These scenes form a thematic core in the novels and share three common characteristics. First, they are modelled on the biblical friendship of David and Jonathan and not, as in works by practising and more reticent homosexuals, on the Greek ideal of male love (Lawrence has other uses for *The Symposium*). The clearest example of Lawrence's version of this male friendship appears in the play about his namesake, *David* (1926), where the two heroes swear an almost divine covenant:

> *Jonathan:* We have sworn a covenant, is it not between us? Wilt thou not swear with me, that our souls shall be as brothers, closer even than the blood? O David, my heart has no peace save all be well between thy soul and mine, and thy blood and mine.
> *David:* As the Lord liveth, the soul of Jonathan is dearer to me than a brother's. — O brother, if I were but come out of this pass, and we might live before the Lord, together![1]

Secondly, in each of these scenes homosexuality is seen as an alternative to heterosexual love and invariably occurs after a frustrating humiliation with a woman. The failure of the male to achieve dominance over the female, especially the female *will*, leads directly to a triumph of the female element *within* man. Thirdly, Lawrence's inner struggle with repressed homosexual desires results in an ambiguity of presentation, for none of his heroes can commit himself completely to homosexuality although it is portrayed as a 'higher' form of sexual love. Though this ambiguity has artistic functions — it deflects attention from the physical to the symbolic aspects of the scene — it also exposes Lawrence's personal doubts about the ultimate validity of homosexual experience. Homosexual lovers like the Prussian Officer, Banford in 'The Fox', Winifred Inger in *The Rainbow* and Loerke in *Women in Love* are portrayed as perverse and corrupt. Yet the homosexuality in the four scenes is described as nourishing and life-enhancing, and represents a meaningful and valuable relationship. Like T. E. Lawrence, who contrasts the clean embraces of the Bedouin with the syphilitic sodomy of the Turks, D. H. Lawrence has contradictory attitudes about inversion.

In letters and conversations with friends, and in his non-fiction, especially his essays on Whitman (he destroyed his homosexual treatise, 'Goats and Compasses', in 1917), Lawrence attempts to clarify his ambiguous position. In 1913 he writes to Henry Savage:

> I should like to know why nearly every man that approaches greatness tends to homosexuality, whether he admits it or not: so that he loves the *body* of a man better than the body of a woman — as I believe the Greeks did, sculptors and all, by far . . . He can

always get satisfaction from a man, but it is the hardest thing in life to get one's soul and body satisfied from a woman, so that one is free from oneself. And one is kept by all tradition and instinct from loving men, or a man.[2]

Lawrence, himself 'approaching greatness', characteristically uses ambiguous language ('*tends* to homosexuality'). The first sentence is similar to Oscar Wilde's defence at his trial, the second affirms the superiority of male to female love, and the third places tradition *with* instinct as obstacles to male love when in his case (and in Wilde's) instinct opposes tradition.

In a letter of 1919 Lawrence seems to have found an answer in Whitman, who with his English disciple Edward Carpenter, was the greatest public apologist for homosexuality:

> You are a great admirer of Whitman. So am I. But I find in his *'Calamus'* and Comrades one of the clues to a real solution — the new adjustment. I believe in what he calls 'manly love', the real implicit reliance of one man on another: as sacred a unison as marriage: only it must be deeper, more ultimate than emotion and personality, cool separateness and yet the ultimate reliance.[3]

These ideas are close to the ideas of *Women in Love*, which he completed a few years earlier in 1916. Lawrence values separateness and feels sexual relations with women threaten his integrity, so that male love is a 'real solution' to the struggle for dominance and conflict of wills in heterosexual love, and comradeship is justified as being as sacred as marriage. But Lawrence writes of Whitman, a practising homosexual:

> He found, as all men find, that you can't really merge in a woman, though you may go a long way. You can't manage the last bit. So you have to give it up, and try elsewhere if you *insist* on merging . . . For the great mergers, woman at last becomes inadequate. For those who love to extremes. Woman is inadequate for the last merging. So the next step is the merging of man-for-man love. And this is on the brink of death. It slides over into death. David and Jonathan. And the death of Jonathan.[4]

The paradox of Whitman's real solution is that the merging of men goes beyond women — but into a sexual dead end, into masturbation and sterility.

During his stay in New Mexico Lawrence again tried to clarify this problem:

> All my life I have wanted friendship with a man — real friendship, in my sense of what I mean by that word. What is this sense? Do I want friendliness? I should like to see anybody being 'friendly' with me. Intellectual equals? Or rather equals in being non-intellectual. I see your joke. Not something homosexual, surely? Indeed, you have misunderstood me — besides this term is so imbedded in its own period. I do not belong to a world where that word has meaning. Comradeship perhaps? No, not that — too much love about it — no, not even in the Calamus sense, not comradeship — not manly love. Then what Nietzsche describes — the friend in whom the world standeth complete, a capsule of the good — the creating friend, who hath always a complete world to bestow. Well, in a way. That means in my words, choose as your friend the man who has centre.[5]

Lawrence rejects in turn intellectual equality, homosexuality in the Wildean sense (imbedded in its period), and Whitman's comradeship for a vague and unsatisfactory definition by Nietzsche, who was betrayed by his friends and whose desperate sexual struggle ended in madness. Lawrence's homosexuality remains: 'I do believe in friendship. I believe tremendously in friendship between man and man, a pledging of men to each other inviolably. But I have not ever met or formed such a friendship.'[6] But his deep residue of puritanical repression and certain intellectual scruples prevent the successful culmination of this friendship.

Yet Lawrence condemned in others what he wanted for himself. 'Never bring Birrell to see me any more', he writes to David Garnett. 'There is something nasty about him like black beetles. He is horrible and unclean. I feel I should go mad when I think of your set, Duncan Grant and Keynes and Birrell. It makes me dream of beetles . . . It sent me mad with misery and hostility and rage.'[7] Nor would Lawrence in his extreme rage, inspired partly by the hatred of the homosexual element within himself, allow the validity of heterosexual love, at least as it was practised by middle- or upper-class Anglo-Saxons. He sees it as disguised perversion:

> That is what nearly *all* English people now do. When a man takes a woman, he is *merely* repeating a known reaction upon himself,

not seeking a new reaction, a discovery. And this is like self-abuse or masturbation. The ordinary Englishman of the educated class goes to a woman now to masturbate himself . . . When this condition arrives, there is always Sodomy.[8]

And in a bitter poem in the aptly named *Pansies*, Lawrence completely loses his objectivity and projects his own 'instinctual' sexual fears on to the class he had come to hate:

Ronald you know, is like most Englishmen,
by instinct he's a sodomist
but he's frightened to know it
so he takes it out on women.

Oh come! said I. That Don Juan of a Ronald! —
Exactly, she said. Don Juan was another of them, in love with
    himself
and taking it out on women —
Even that isn't sodomitical, said I
But if a man is in love with himself, isn't that the meanest form of
    homosexuality? she said.[9]

I. THE WHITE PEACOCK

The character based on Lawrence's father dies at the beginning of early works like *The White Peacock* and 'Odour of Chrysanthemums', and it is not until *Sons and Lovers* (1914) that Walter Morel appears in his frightening reality. Yet Mr Beardsall, who abandons his family and returns only to die an alcoholic death, plays a minor but significant role in *The White Peacock*. For the passionate dissatisfaction of Mr and Mrs Beardsall is the model for two other disastrous marriages in the novel: of Annable and his first 'superior' wife (which predicts what the marriage of George and Lettie would have been like), and of George and Meg. (In the same way, Lettie, who detests yet marries the 'mean fop' Leslie, foreshadows the fate of Alice, who marries an old acquaintance who had been her particular aversion.) George, who is drunk when he proposes to Meg, degenerates from a healthy animalism to an alcoholism similar to Mr Beardsall's; and Cyril is able to give George the final comfort that Cyril failed to give his father — whom he did not recognize in their brief meeting before his death.

The degraded and degenerate Mr Beardsall stands at one extreme among the male characters of the novel who form a symbolic representation of the descent of man from the over-refined to the barbarian — from Cyril and Leslie to George, Annable and Beardsall — in which the cultured men lack passion and the passionate men renounce culture. Mr Beardsall's death, Annable's fatal accident and even Leslie's minor disaster seem to clear the field for Cyril and George. Cyril's physical attraction to the rugged masculinity of George and Annable is an attempt to break away from his possessive mother, who 'hated my father before I was born', and regain his lost father. His sexual debilitation (he constantly urges George to sexual aggression with his sister, Lettie, but can never act himself) suits him for the passive role as narrator-voyeur.

Lettie is afraid of sex with George but not with Leslie, for when their lovemaking is interrupted, 'Lettie followed, tidying her hair. She did not laugh and look confused, as most girls do on similar occasions'.[10] But the dangerous, threatening passion of George and Lettie can be ignited merely by the spark of Maurice Greiffenhagen's *An Idyll* (1891), a painting that had great significance for Lawrence and which plays an important symbolic role in the novel.[11]

In this painting a swarthy Pan figure, of great vigour and vitality, bare-chested and clothed in animal skins, seems rooted in a meadow where the grazing sheep and olive trees are lit up by a setting sun. He is lifting a pale, Pre-Raphaelite young woman off her feet, which are covered with bright poppies and daisies. He presses her half-naked bosom against his own body, entwines his fingers in the thick auburn hair cascading down her blue garment to her buttocks, and kisses her cheek as she turns away and swoons limply in his muscular arms, half-afraid of passion. Cyril's remark (a characteristic Laurentian complaint) is an excellent gloss on the painting: 'A woman is so ready to disclaim the body of a man's love; she yields him her own soft beauty with so much gentle patience and regret; she clings to his neck . . . shrinking from his passionate limbs and his body' (317).

George admires the painting, which rouses him sexually, but Lettie's ironic-defensive response is: 'She may well be half afraid, when the barbarian comes out in his glory, skins and all . . . Make love to the *next girl* you meet, and . . . she'll have need to be more than half afraid.' Yet when George hesitates and 'insists' (in the subjunctive), 'I don't know whether I should like any girl I know to —', Lettie mocks him and says he ought to have been a monk or a martyr instead of a satyr. George glances at her breasts, shivers, and attempts to make small talk, for 'It was a torture to each of them to look thus nakedly at the other, a dazzled, shrinking pain that they forced themselves to undergo for a moment, that they might the moment after tremble with a fierce sensation that filled their veins with fluid, fiery electricity' (43-4). The painting reveals the emotions that they cannot and dare not express.

This scene of barely restrained passion is repeated thrice in the novel: in the dance, the wood and the swim. Though the novel is seriously flawed by an awkward narrator who cannot possibly have seen all he reports, by an unfocused plot, by two gratuitous accidents, and by a superfluity of wounded and bloody animals that are meant to suggest, as in Hardy, that 'life seems so terrible', Lawrence nevertheless shows considerable skill in his presentation of the four scenes that express the frustration of love. When George and Lettie fail to find emotional fulfilment or sexual realization, he marries the earthy Meg, who can satisfy his body but not his mind; and she marries Leslie, who provides mental but not physical satisfaction and who, in a fetishistic moment (the reverse of *An Idyll*) kneels down and rubs her cold feet while she touches his cheek and calls him 'dear boy'. George's obstacle is class, and the plot of the novel is similar to *Wuthering Heights*, where Catherine marries the stiff Linton instead of the passionate Heathcliff.

George's riotous dance with Lettie is the second scene of sublimated sexual passion. Mr Saxton shouts for them to stop.

But George continued the dance; her hair was shaken loose, and fell in a great coil down her back; her feet began to drag; you could hear a light slur on the floor; she was panting — I could see her lips murmur to him, begging him to stop; he was laughing with open mouth, holding her tight; at last her feet trailed; he lifted her, clasping her tightly, and danced twice round the room with her thus. Then he fell with a crash on the sofa, pulling her beside him. His eyes glowed like coals; he was panting in sobs, and his hair was wet and glistening. She lay back on the sofa, with his arm still around her, not moving; she was quite overcome. Her hair was wild about her face. (115)

The powerful rhythms approximate Dionysian music as well as sexual movements and end in the climactic exhaustion of a sexual orgasm. This scene also repeats in a subtle way the sexual posture of *An Idyll*: the man's glowing look as he lifts and tightly clasps the woman, and the woman's loose hair, parted lips, trailing feet and attitude of fearful yet passionate abandon.

Even after they are both engaged, George cannot give up Lettie, and in the wood that recalls the pastoral background of *An Idyll*, he vainly pleads for her love and once again re-enacts the emotions of the painting: 'She turned and kissed him gratefully. He then took her in a long, passionate embrace, mouth to mouth. In the end it had so wearied her, that she could only wait in his arms till he was too tired to hold her. He was trembling already' (248).

The swimming scene is the culmination of the novel (after it the characters listlessly follow their predestined fate) and is a synthesis not only of the idyllic passion of the dance and the wood, but also of the story of Annable's first marriage. When Annable was courting his wife, he used to swim in the river and 'dry myself on the bank full where she might see me . . . I was Greek statues for her'. Annable, like George, was a poor young man, was called *son boeuf* (Lettie calls George *'bos-bovis'*), and suffers sexual humiliation. Annable openly expresses George's more covert hostility to women, and the titular white male peacock, who dirties the head of an angel statue and symbolizes the soul of woman, 'all vanity and screech and defilement', represents Lettie as well as Annable's Lady Chrystabel. In Lawrence's novels, frustrated passion and frustrating marriage lead inevitably to a moment of male love.

The swimming scene takes place immediately after Lettie's final rejection of George during the third idyll in the wood, and at the end of Cyril's tepid and unsuccessful courtship of George's sister, Emily. Cyril, who is sometimes called Sybil, longs for some one to nestle against, and his strong attachment to George during the hay harvest culminates in the Whitmanesque 'Poem of Friendship' where the naked men roll in the grass and frolic in the pond, and the faithful dog chases away the intruding Emily.[12] A bit earlier, George is sexually excited by looking at Cyril's reproductions of the effeminate Beardsley's *Atalanta* and *Salome*: 'the more I look at these naked lines, the more I want her. It's a sort of fine sharp feeling, like these curved lines'[13] (187). And at the pond, as Cyril *Beardsall* admires George's naked body, George 'laughed at me, telling me I was like one of Aubrey *Beardsley's* long, lean ugly fellows. I referred him to many classic examples of slenderness', in the same way that Annable compared himself to Greek statues. And as Cyril loses himself in contemplation of George's physical beauty, he remembers the story of Annable. George

> saw I had forgotten to continue my rubbing, and laughing he took hold of me and began to rub me briskly, as if I were a child, or rather, a woman he loved and did not fear. I left myself quite limply in his hands, and, to get a better grip of me, he put his arm round me and pressed me against him, and the sweetness of the touch of our naked bodies one against the other was superb. It satisfied in some measure the vague, indecipherable yearning of my soul; and it was the same with him. When he had rubbed me all warm, he let me go, and we looked at each other with eyes of still laughter, and our love was perfect for a moment, more perfect than any love I have known since, either for man or woman.[14] (257)

The 'rubbing' is explicitly homosexual as Cyril replaces his tall and threatening sister Lettie (just as George replaces Emily for Cyril), and becomes 'a woman he loved and did not fear' in this final representation of the limp, passive figure pressed against the powerful male in *An Idyll*. The feeble rationalization ('to get a better grip') for the 'naked bodies one against the other' only heightens the homosexual effect, which to the reader is far from 'vague and indecipherable'. We are not told what George feels, but Cyril projects his own feelings on to his lover ('it was the same with him'). The frank, lyrical look 'with eyes of still laughter' is a satisfying contrast to George and Lettie's torture 'to look thus nakedly at the other'. Cyril's final statement is a paraphrase of David's lament for Jonathan in II Samuel 1: 26, 'very pleasant hast thou been unto me: thy love to me was wonderful, passing the love of women'. In the 'Poem of Friendship', the Whitmanesque and biblical motifs combine to form a satisfying homosexual idyll the contrasts with unhappy marriages and frustrated love.

II. WOMEN IN LOVE

Just as *The White Peacock* is directly related to Lawrence's family situation, so *Women in Love* grows out of his sexual struggles with Frieda Weekley and his attempts at male friendship, especially with Middleton Murry. Throughout his entire life Lawrence felt threatened by dominating or possessive women: his mother, Jessie Chambers, Alice Dax, Lady Ottoline Morrell, Dorothy Brett, Mabel Dodge Luhan and, most important, Frieda, and from his experience with them he learned to see heterosexual love as an endless struggle of clashing wills in which man either maintains a precarious dominance or is overcome by humiliating defeat.

Though Lawrence kept up his end of the battle, as the scarifying *Look, We Have Come Through!* testifies, he had much to fear from Frieda, whose strengths seemed to match his weaknesses. She was of noble birth, richer, older, stronger and healthier than the sickly Lawrence; she was sexually liberated and had a number of love affairs before, during and after her marriages to Ernest Weekley and the puritanical Lorenzo. He resented his dependence on Frieda, was awed by her sexual experience and sexual demands, was fiercely jealous of the longing for her three abandoned children (they had no children of their own), hated her wilful refusal to submit to him, and was alternately enraged, depressed and resigned to her flirtations and liaisons. For Lawrence,

> The cross,
> The wheel on which our silence first is broken, [is]
> Sex, which breaks up our integrity, our single inviolability, our
>   deep silence,
> Tearing a cry from us.[15]

It was therefore inevitable that Lawrence had sexual problems with Frieda and, as Murry writes, sought 'to escape to a man from the misery of his own failure with a woman'.[16] Several of Lawrence's other 'friends' have also attempted to diagnose his sexual difficulties. Compton Mackenzie records, in a patronizing tone, that

> What worried him particularly was his inability to attain consummation simultaneously with his wife, which according to

him must mean that their marriage was still imperfect in spite of all they had both gone through. I insisted that such a happy coincidence was always rare, but he became more and more depressed about what *he* insisted was the only evidence of a perfect union. 'I believe that the nearest I've ever come to perfect love was with a young coal-miner when I was about sixteen,' he declared.[17]

And Cecil Gray, whom Lawrence satirized as Cyril Scott in *Aaron's Rod*, hints about an affair with Frieda[18] and categorically states: 'It might not be true to say that Lawrence was literally and absolutely impotent . . . but I am certain that he was not very far removed from it'.[19] The basis of Gray's 'certainty' is not explained, but it is clear that Lawrence was not impotent if he experienced orgasms.

Whatever the validity of these waspish accounts, Lawrence's marriage suffered two major crises: one culminating in Cornwall in 1916 during the composition of *Women in Love*, the other in Mexico in 1923 when writing *The Plumed Serpent*. In the first crisis Lawrence turned away from Frieda toward Rananim in general and Murry in particular. Knud Merrild writes:

> When he spoke of his beloved idea of starting a new life and forming a colony, he never included women. He always conceived of realizing it with men alone, in the beginning at least . . . Only at times he added, 'I suppose eventually the men shall want to take women unto themselves!' . . .
> There is no use blinking the fact that Lawrence included the possibility of homosexuality in the scheme of modern existence, that he offered it as a tentative relief from an antagonism between the sexes, a symptom of a disease that has spread over Europe.[20]

The sexually naïve Murry, who agreed with Lawrence's accusation that he lacked a sensuous nature, was confused and overwhelmed by the intensity of his friend's passion — 'Lawrence was really a new experience. I was quite unprepared for such an immediacy of contact.' So he had to resort to role-playing: 'When he consciously sought for *me*, expecting response from me, the same uneasy bewilderment would return. The person to whom he spoke was not there: I must impersonate him.'[21] Gradually, however,

Murry came to understand and accept the ambivalent and even contradictory elements in Lawrence's creed:

> One was an instinctive, infra-personal sense of solidarity with men — the true, deep, gregarious experience, which Lawrence had known as a child and longed to renew, which he simultaneously desired and repudiated; the other was a curiously intense preoccupation with 'the animal of himself,' which fascinated and repelled him[22]

(as it did Murry). But Lawrence's need corresponded to Murry's, for Murry was also having serious problems in his marriage to Katherine Mansfield. In the early years of the war, writes Murry: 'By far the chief among [my desires] was the desire to live in a warm atmosphere of love. At this time it existed between Lawrence and me, and I would do anything not to break it.'[23] And he describes their perfect union in words that repeat David's lament for Jonathan and Cyril's paean in 'The Poem of Friendship': 'We did not have to, we did not want to, talk; it was good between us, better than I have ever known with a living man'.[24]

But their friendship degenerated when Katherine quite naturally resented Lawrence's assaults on her marriage and his attempt to regenerate it through his passionate attachment to her husband:

> Lawrence believed, or tried to believe, that the relation between Katherine and me was false and deadly; and that the relation between Frieda and himself was real and life-giving: but that this relation with Frieda needed to be completed by a new relation between himself and me, which I evaded . . . By virtue of this 'mystical' relation with Lawrence, I participate in this pre-elemental reality, and the 'dark sources' of my being come alive. From this changed personality, I, in turn, enter a new relation with Katherine.[25]

The emotional yet abstract language does not explain precisely why Lawrence needs completion or how the Murrys recharge themselves on Lawrence's marital battery, but it is not difficult to see how these ideas offended Katherine. When Murry tried to placate Lawrence in Cornwall in 1916 by asking, 'If I love you, and you know I love you, isn't that enough?', Lorenzo burst out, 'I hate your love, I *hate* it. You're an obscene bug, *sucking* my life away',[26] an insult that combined his favourite image of corruption with the suggestion of perversion. Lawrence's response to the inevitable break with Murry was his mysterious and obscure passion for the handsome Cornish farmer, William Henry Hocking, which he refers to in the 'Nightmare' chapter of *Kangaroo* (1923) and in the suppressed Prologue to *Women in Love*, which was not published until 1963.[27]

The Prologue concerns three crucial aspects of the novel: the early history of Birkin's destructive relationship with Hermione that explains her violent attempt to crush his skull with the lapis lazuli; the friendship, intimacy and attraction of Birkin and Crich that begins on an Alpine journey and clarifies Birkin's final lament: 'He should have loved me . . . I wanted eternal union with a man too: another kind of love.' But Ursula calls this desire a perversity, for it negates Birkin's commitment to female love:

> In the street, it was the men who roused him by their flesh and their manly, vigorous movement, quite apart from all the individual character, whilst he studied the women as *sisters*, knowing their meaning and their intents. It was the men's physique which held the passion and the mystery to him . . . He had several friendships wherein this passion entered . . . He loved his friend, the beauty of whose manly limbs made him tremble with pleasure. He wanted to caress him.[28]

Thirdly, the revelation of Birkin's repressed homosexual desires (which accounts for the cancellation of the Prologue, especially after the suppression of *The Rainbow*, with its lesbian swimming scene), clarifies the 'Man to Man' and 'Gladiatorial' chapters:

> This was the one and only secret he kept to himself, this secret of his passionate and sudden, spasmatic affinity for the men he saw. He kept this secret even from himself . . . Gerald Crich was the one towards whom Birkin felt most strongly that immediate, roused attraction which transfigured the person of the attracter with such a glow and such a desirable beauty.[29]

Birkin's open desires and homosexual affairs with working men, in the Prologue, have a rather different emphasis from the analogous description at the end of Chapter 2 where Birkin and Crich

> burned with each other, inwardly. This they would never admit. They intended to keep their relationship a casual free-and-easy

friendship, they were not going to be so unmanly and unnatural
as to allow any heart-burning between them. They had not the
faintest belief in deep relationship between men and men, and
their disbelief prevented any development of their powerful but
suppressed friendliness.[30]

This passage is more covert and defensive, even ironic ('unmanly',
'heart-burning'); and Lawrence's uneasiness with this intensely
personal theme is revealed as the novel thrusts toward — not away
from — the development of their 'suppressed friendliness'.

Just before this passage Birkin tells Crich, 'It's the hardest thing in
the world to act spontaneously on one's impulses', and his revulsion
from Hermione in the Prologue suggests what his deepest impulses
really are. In the novel too Birkin is threatened not only by
Hermione's bullying, clutching, powerful will, but also by Ursula's
horrible, assertive 'lust for possession, a greed for self-importance in
love'. The violent hostility between men and women erupts
throughout the novel: in Hermione's attack, Mino's cuff, Gudrun's
slap, Mr Brangwen's smack and Crich's strangulation. Even when
Birkin and Ursula's love is relatively successful, Birkin fears his loss
of sexual identity in submergence and 'horrible fusion':

> On the whole, he hated sex, it was such a limitation. It was sex
> that turned a man into a broken half of a couple, the woman into
> the other broken half. And he wanted to be single in himself, the
> woman single in herself. He wanted sex to revert to the level of,
> the other appetites, to be regarded as a functional process, not as a
> fulfilment . . . Why should we consider ourselves, men and
> women, as broken fragments of one whole? . . . In the old age,
> before sex was, we were mixed, each one a mixture. The process
> of singling into individuality resulted in the great polarization of
> sex. The womanly drew to one side, the manly to the other. But
> the separation was imperfect even then (223, 225).

This is Lawrence's interpretation of the platonic theory of physical
love. In *The Symposium* Aristophanes explains Love by supposing
that 'the primeval man ['in the old age, before sex was'] was round
and had four hands and four feet, back and sides forming a circle, one
head with two faces', and was subsequently divided into two. After
the division, the two parts of man, each desiring his other half, came

together, and threw their arms about one another eager to grow into one. Plato's theory is appealing because it explains the attraction of the sexes and shows that the union of masculine and feminine complements is a return to original wholeness. But in Lawrence's version the polarized broken half, frightened of merging and domination, wants to remain single and never experiences the platonic fulfilment with women. Birkin yearns for a starlike 'equilibrium, a pure balance of single beings', but Ursula immediately recognizes that what he really wants is a satellite, a woman submissive to his will. And when woman refuses to submit, he moves away from the *pis aller* of marriage, from the *égoisme à deux*, towards the idealistic and never-to-be-achieved 'bond of pure trust and love with the other man'.

Right after his confession that he hates sex, Birkin first realizes what was apparent in the Prologue: that 'he had been loving Gerald all along, and all along denying it'. So he proposes a *Blutbrüderschaft* to Crich who, doomed and limited, denies his animal self and begs to 'leave it till I understand it better'. Just as Birkin's archaic proposal comes from dissatisfaction with Ursula so, as Murry writes in an interesting comment on this scene, Lawrence's

> relation with Frieda left room, and perhaps need, for a relation with a man of something of the kind and quality of my relation with Katherine; and he wanted this relation with me. It was possible only if it left my relation with Katherine intact.

But Lawrence threatened Murry's marriage, and wanted to control his body and dominate his mind.

> So at this critical moment, I began to withdraw towards Katherine. And as he felt my withdrawal, Lawrence became more urgent to bind me with him. He talked of the blood-brotherhood between us, and hinted at the need of some inviolable sacrament between us — some pre-Christian blood-rite in keeping with the primeval [Cornish] rocks about us . . . No doubt the queer wrestling-match between the two [Birkin and Crich] is more or less what he meant by the 'blood-sacrament' between us.[31]

Though there is no male blood-rite with Birkin, Gerald achieves a *Blutschwesterschaft* with Gudrun, first when he spurs his mare at the railway crossing and nearly brings Gudrun to orgasm, and then when the frenzied rabbit, Bismarck, scores their arms with blood. Bismarck symbolizes the two forms of destructive love that Gudrun experiences with Crich and with Loerke. The rabbit's racing round and round its cage 'like a furry meteorite, in a tense hard circle that seemed to bind their brains' (273) represents the mindless Dionysian ecstasy ('It's like going round in a squirrel cage', 283) that Gudrun achieves with Crich. Gudrun reads Prince Bismarck's letters in the Alps, and Bismarck's countryman, Loerke, depicts 'whirling ridiculously in roundabouts . . . a frenzy of chaotic motion' in his industrial frieze based on Mark Gertler's painting, *Merry-Go-Round* (1916).

Birkin attacks this Dionysian ecstasy in the 'Moony' chapter that follows 'Rabbit', and his impossible attempt to break the image of the moon that 'shook upon the water in triumphant reassumption' symbolizes his desire to destroy Ursula's female power, to shatter her spiritual integrity. 'Like the moon, one half of [Hermione] was lost to life', but Ursula survives Birkin's attempt to violate her and leads him back toward wholeness. The following day, inspired by his love for Ursula, Birkin proposes marriage; and when this ends in a comical fiasco he turns to Crich for consolation and makes another proposal: 'let us strip, and do it properly'.

Birkin's confession that he used to wrestle with a Jap is his metaphorical revelation of homosexual experience, for Japs 'Repel and attract, both. They are very repulsive when they are cold . . . But when they are hot and roused, there is a definite attraction.'

So the two men began to struggle together . . . They seemed to drive their white flesh deeper and deeper against each other, as if they would break into a oneness . . . It was as if Birkin's whole physical intelligence interpenetrated into Gerald's body, as if his fine, sublimated energy entered into the flesh of the fuller man, like some potency . . . Now and again came a sharp gasp of breath, or a sound like a sigh, then the rapid thudding of movement on the thickly-carpeted floor, then the strange sound of flesh escaping under flesh . . . The physical junction of two bodies clinched into oneness . . .

At length Gerald lay back inert on the carpet, his breast rising in great slow panting, whilst Birkin kneeled over him, almost unconscious. Birkin was much more exhausted. He caught little,·

short breaths, he could scarcely breathe any more. The earth seemed to tilt and sway, and a complete darkness was coming over his mind . . . The world was sliding, everything was sliding off into the darkness. And he was sliding, endlessly, endlessly away. (304-5)

Birkin and Crich, by penetrating and entering the flesh and experiencing mutual excitement, achieve a platonic oneness that they fail to achieve in heterosexual love. Just as the less passionate and less explicit 'Poem of Friendship' was exalted by a biblical allusion to David and Jonathan, so this almost religious scene alludes to Jacob wrestling with the angel of God in Genesis 32:24-30: 'And Jacob was left alone; and there a man wrestled with him until the breaking of the day . . . And Jacob called the name of the place Peniel: for I have seen God face to face, and my life is preserved.'[32] Birkin tells Crich 'you are beautiful' and Crich confesses: 'I don't believe I've ever felt as much *love* for a woman as I have for you — not *love*'.

Though they seem completely fulfilled, one significant detail qualifies their union and links their perversity with the Bohemian set of Halliday and Minette. When they wake from sleep Crich puts on 'a gown of broad-barred, thick black-and-green silk, brilliant and striking', and this gown is similar to the colourful one Minette wears ('a loose dressing-gown of purple silk', 84) just before she sleeps with Crich in Halliday's flat. When Crich wakes after sleeping with his host's pregnant mistress and puts on his 'silk wrap of a beautiful bluish colour, with an amethyst hem', he is surprised to find Halliday and Libidnikov (corruption and libido?) stark naked in front of the fire (which also burns during the wrestling match). At that moment Crich first overcomes his bodily shame and repulsion, and returns from his bath without clothes. This change prepares him for the wrestling scene.

Despite their complete satisfaction, neither Crich nor Birkin can entirely commit himself to homosexuality. Crich chooses a love with Gudrun that is doomed to frozen disaster as much as any love in Hardy;[33] and Birkin again demands Ursula's total submission while she accuses him of perverse and obscene sex with Hermione. The sexual solution, as far as the novel admits of one, comes in 'Excurse'.

The sexual transfiguration of Birkin and Ursula is again presented in biblical terms and compared to the Sons of God taking the fair daughters of men (Genesis 6:2) and to Moses smiting the rock in Horeb with his rod so 'there shall come water out of it, that the people may drink' (Exodus 17:6). At the country inn Birkin and Ursula reach the fundamental

> source of the deepest life-force, the darkest, deepest, strangest life-source of the human body, at the back and base of the loins . . . From the smitten rock of the man's body, from the strange marvellous flanks and thighs, deeper, further in mystery than the phallic source, came the floods of ineffable darkness and ineffable riches. (354)

Later in the novel Ursula remembers the freedom achieved through her 'degrading, bestial and shameful' experiences with Birkin.[34] In this passage Lawrence equates anal intercourse (the back and the base of the loins, beyond the phallic source) with the deepest life-source, but he describes the heterosexuality of Gudrun and Crich as 'the terrible frictional violence of death'.

The equation of the anus with the life source is such an obscene and outrageous idea that some of the most perceptive critics have either ignored it entirely or else refused to face the full implications of Lawrence's homosexuality. Spilka believes that male friendship is 'the step beyond marriage which makes marriage possible, the break-through to a fuller life'.[35] 'Birkin must work through his "living desire" for Gerald, as well as his deathly attachment to Hermione, before he can love Ursula "body and soul" '.[36] But could a wife ever accept a man's claim that he would be a better husband if he practised sodomy?

Goodheart more realistically states that Birkin's 'search for transcendent states of being . . . draws him away from women, not toward them . . . Birkin suffers from a homosexual fear of women',[37] but he does not emphasize Birkin's corresponding attraction for men. Daleski says more precisely that 'the distinct homosexual colouring of the description of the wrestling bout . . . is evidence of the pronounced feminine component in his make-up, of a latent or repressed homosexual tendency, rather than any overt homosexual intention on his part',[38] but the homosexuality in 'Gladiatorial' *is* overt. And Spilka again takes the most naïve view of Birkin's buggery with Ursula: Birkin 'can even perform "responsibly" the kind of "bestial" act he might have performed with a man and perhaps did perform with Hermione — and feel liberated by it ("he was so unabashed and unrestrained") rather than degraded'.[39] These interpretations, like many of Lawrence's own pronouncements about sex, fail to reconcile the abysmal gap between sexual idealism and sexual reality.[40] For the sexual struggles in *Women in Love* (and in Lawrence's life) exemplify his disturbing statement in 'The Reality of Peace': 'It is not of love that we are fulfilled, but of love in such intimate equipoise with hate that the transcendence takes place'.[41]

The anal intercourse in 'Excurse' is compounded of such love and hate. By denying Ursula's female integrity and her sexuality (as he did in 'Moony') and by penetrating her anus, Birkin uses Ursula as a sexual substitute for Crich and does to her what he wants to do to Gerald. But Birkin's own actions belie his assertion that if Crich 'pledged himself with the man he would later be able to pledge himself with the woman: not merely in legal marriage, but in absolute mystic marriage', for Birkin never actually abandons homosexuality. By substituting anal marriage for inversion, he sublimates and satisfies his desires in an alternative and perhaps even more perverse way.[42]

III. AARON'S ROD

Like Cyril and Birkin, Aaron is a covert homosexual who cannot finally commit himself to male love. In all three novels the hero vacillates indecisively between hetero- and homosexual love: Cyril is attracted to both Emily and George, Birkin to Ursula and Crich, Aaron to the Marchesa and Lilly. But unlike Cyril who renounces Emily and drifts away from George, or Birkin whose passion for Crich is superseded by anal intercourse with Ursula, Aaron has three disastrous relationships with women.

Aaron is highly sexed but extremely repressed, and finds it hard to endure life 'without desire, without any movement of passionate love, only gripped back in recoil!'[43] The 'thought of any loving, any real sort of coming together between himself and anybody' is objectionable, so that all his mad loving is only a willed, mechanical effort (174). When Aaron secretly watches his wife, Lottie, just before he deserts her, he feels completely enervated: 'He felt weak, like a drowning man who acquiesces in the waters. His strength was gone, he was sinking back. He would sink back to it all, float henceforth like a drowned man' (37). His sex life with Lottie is a failure, for he projects his fears on to her and then blames her for them. Aaron sees marriage as a deadlock of fixed, tense wills and refuses to submit to the 'extreme of self-abandon in love'. He 'never wanted to surrender himself utterly to Lottie: nor to his mother: nor to anybody' and sink into the 'degeneration of slime and merge' (161-2). (This single reference to Aaron's mother suggests that fears of his mother are mingled and confused with fears of his wife.) So Aaron runs away from his first woman to play his flute in a London orchestra.

His friend, Rawdon Lilly, the homosexual propagandist, also has serious marital problems. The 'growing *rapprochement*' between Jim Bricknell and Lilly's wife, Tanny, leads to Lilly's jealousy, a punch from Jim that knocks out Lilly's breath, and Tanny's departure for Norway. In *Aaron's Rod* men and women sometimes achieve moments of true understanding and deep knowledge — the Indian doctor with Lottie (as Aaron passively watches), Jim with Tanny (as Lilly watches), and Aaron with the Marchesa (as Del Torre watches) — but husband and wife never do.

While in London, Aaron is sexually pursued by Josephine Ford, Jim's fiancée. At first Aaron refuses to kiss her, but he eventually succumbs to her demands and collapses immediately afterwards in front of Lilly's Covent Garden flat. Aaron, who always kept himself back, attributes his physical breakdown not to the influenza epidemic of 1919, but to his affair with Josephine. 'I gave into her', he explains to Lilly, as if he had contracted venereal and not viral disease, 'and that's what did it. I should have been all right if I hadn't given in to her' (84). (In Florence, Aaron believes he is robbed because he 'got worked up with the Marchesa' and 'exposed himself'.) Aaron is terrified when Lilly wants to call Lottie, gets into his friend's pyjamas and 'goes rotten' in his soul.

In order to 'rouse Aaron up' Lilly says, 'I'm going to rub you with oil. I'm going to rub you as mothers do their babies whose bowels don't work', although Aaron is not constipated and massaging his genitals would not cure him if he were.

Quickly he uncovered the blond lower body of his patient, and began to rub the abdomen with oil, using a slow, rhythmic, circulating motion, a sort of massage. For a long time he rubbed finely and steadily, then went over the whole of the lower body, mindless, as if in a sort of incantation. He rubbed every speck of the man's lower body — the abdomen, the buttocks, the thighs and knees, down to his feet, rubbed it all and glowing with camphorated oil, every bit of it, chafing the toes swiftly, till he was almost exhausted. Then Aaron was covered up again, and Lilly sat down in fatigue to look at his patient.

He saw a change. The spark had come back into the sick eyes, and the faint trace of a smile, faintly luminous, into the face. Aaron was regaining himself. But Lilly said nothing. He watched his patient fall into a proper sleep. (91)[44]

The rhythmic, incantatory, metaphoric and repetitive (the whole, every speck, every bit) quality of this passage should not distract from the literal meaning, especially since Lilly darns Aaron's socks, talks like a woman, and serves him like a housemaid ('the lily toils and spins hard enough, in her own way').[45] And in a violent fit of revulsion against his wife's refusal to submit to him (women 'all prefer to kick against the pricks. Not that *they* get many pricks. I get them', 91), Lilly joins his revived friend in a corrosive condemnation of women. Aaron complains, 'They want to get you under and children is their chief weapon . . . I want my own pleasure, or nothing: and children be damned', to which Lilly adds, with a significant phrase, 'And can you find two men *to stick together* without feeling criminal, and without cringing, and without betraying one another? You can't. One is sure to go fawning round some female, then they both enjoy giving each other away, and doing a new grovel before a woman again' (96).

Their rather unusual fear of being used as an instrument of propagation explains Lawrence's insane tirade against the vermin 'who teem by the billion, like the Chinese and Japs and Orientals altogether . . . Even niggers are better than Asiatics, though they are wallowers' (92). If 'higher types breed slower', then the less breeding the higher the type. Thus, the breeder Aaron abandons his children, Lilly has no children, and Lawrence advocates male love that precludes the possibility of propagation. (In *Women in Love* Birkin practises a form of intercourse which effectively prevents the kind of unwanted pregnancy that resulted from Ursula's 'perverse' relations with Skrebensky in *The Rainbow*.)

The nursing scene is also based on a crucial moment in the friendship of Lawrence and Murry. In February 1915 Murry, abandoned by Katherine Mansfield who ran off to her lover in France, arrived in Greatham to visit Lawrence. During the long walk from the station Murry's cold turned to influenza and Lawrence devoted himself to nursing his friend. Murry says that 'Lawrence bundled me straight into bed and kept me there for two days, looking after me as though I were a child';[46] and Lawrence told Ottoline Morrell, 'At present he is my partner — the only man who is quite simply with me'.[47] The opportunity to give strength and comfort to the ailing Murry was particularly important to Lawrence, for he and Katherine Mansfield were tubercular just as Frieda and Murry were usually healthy, and this moment afforded Lawrence a gratifying reversal of his weaker and more passive role. According to Murry, Lilly's rubbing of Aaron provided the 'crucial physical contact which was, for Lawrence, a necessary and essential part of the relation between man and man'. Just as Lawrence seeks a homosexual union with Murry 'because he finds it impossible to achieve sexual fulfilment in marriage',[48] so Lilly desires a homosexual relation with Aaron to complete his marriage with Tanny.

Aaron's rather parasitic relationship with the Bricknells and with Lilly in the first half of the novel is continued with Sir William Franks, Angus and Francis, Algy Constable, the Marchese Del Torre and even James Argyll during his Italian journey. In Florence Aaron becomes friendly with several homosexuals, sleeps with his friend's wife, participates in a second male attack on women, works out the relation between love and power, and returns to Lilly just as his friend is about to return to his wife.

As in *Women in Love*, Lawrence satirizes the homosexual-artistic milieu. Angus and Francis, 'two weird young birds', find Aaron's rod '*perfectly divine*!!!', and patronize him during the journey from Novara to Florence. In the latter Aaron also meets James Argyll, a character obviously based on the homosexual Norman Douglas, who describes himself as 'a shady bird, in all senses of the word', who accuses Del Torre of 'starting with the tail-end' long ago ('Don't play the *ingénue* with me . . . Never believe a woman when she says she's chaste, nor a man when he says he's _____' straight?); who warns the flautist about 'spoiling the shape of your mouth — like Alcibiades', the catamite of Socrates; and who believes that life is 'but a search for a friend'. But Lawrence's caustic portrayal of these men seems to deny the validity of Lilly's homosexual doctrine.

In the 'Nel Paradiso' chapter, which alludes to Dante as well as Argyll's top floor flat, Aaron, Lilly, *Del Torre* and Argyll gaze out at Giotto's phallic belltower, confess their marital and sexual unhappiness, and condemn the terrible will and dominating desires of women in a scene that repeats Aaron and Lilly's earlier attack. In 'paradiso' women are equated with the very hottest inferno. Del Torre, after complaining about his wife's sexual habits (carefully noted by Aaron), expresses a predilection (similar to Loerke's), for young girls who know nothing and 'will be soft and responding to his wishes' (238). This awkward boys-in-the-backroom conversation reaffirms Aaron's need for sexual isolation and his hateful fascination for Lilly (which is similar to Crich's attitude toward Birkin).[49]

But when Aaron tries to escape these disturbing, ambivalent feelings and cuckolds his sexual *confidant* (in his own house and bed), he cannot suppress his instinctive hatred of the Marchesa. In order to get rid of the Marchesa, whose sexual demands begin to threaten him, Aaron makes the absurdly late confession that he is married and loves his wife; and when she surprisingly accepts his explanation, his male pride is severely wounded.

Until the last chapter the relation of the sexual and political themes is subtly handled. Lawrence suggests that the struggle for sexual dominance results in a destructive violence, and that the masses must submit to the 'healthy individual authority' of a leader in the same way that women must submit to men. In the penultimate chapter, when Aaron's rod is shattered by an anarchist bomb, the four different but complementary meanings of the main symbol — rod, flower, flute and penis — fuse into a significant whole. In Numbers 17:8-10, Aaron's rod 'brought forth buds and bloomed blossoms and yielded almonds' and is used as 'a token against the rebels . . . [to] take away their murmurings'. In the novel Lilly refers to the five-foot high phallic flower named after the blossoming rod, but *this* rod is useless against the anarchist rebels. When the bomb destroys the flute, that is, when Aaron is symbolically castrated and has 'to live without a rod', he must renounce his quest for phallic immortality and submit his sexual will to Lilly.

In the last chapter, 'Words', the love and power themes become gratuitously explicit as Lilly again preaches the doctrine that has already been repeated *ad nauseam* throughout the book. Aaron realizes that 'if he had to yield his wilful independence, and give himself, then he would rather give himself to the little, individual *man* than to . . . the quicksands of woman or the stinking bog of society' (280). ('Quicksands' and 'bog' symbolize the 'last great merging' in which the male is swallowed up and disappears.) Lilly discovers Aaron in bed 'like a woman who's had a baby' (an echo of the nursing scene), they walk out to the country past a stream where 'three naked boys still adventurously bathed', and Lilly advises Aaron not to 'kick against the pricks' but to accept them.

The image that Lawrence uses to symbolize triumphant male love is Whitman's 'Dalliance of the Eagles' (David and Jonathan 'were swifter than eagles'): 'Two eagles in mid-air, grappling, whirling, coming to their intensification of love-oneness . . . each·bearing itself up on its own wings at every moment of the mid-air love consummation. That is the splendid love-way'[50] (163). And Lawrence writes that Whitman

> sings of the mystery of manly love, the love of comrades. Over and over he says the same thing: the new world will be built on the love of comrades, the new great dynamic of life will be manly love. Out of this manly love will come the inspiration for the future.[51]

Though the eagle is noble and the idea grand, there is no indication in either Whitman or in Lawrence of *how* the new great dynamic will become the inspiration of the future. Their love of comrades is a personal predilection expressed in poetic language, which obscures the precise meaning as it disguises the perverse reality.

Aaron's Rod has many components of a homosexual novel: three unhappy marriages and two unsuccessful love affairs; an intense hatred and fear of women, who are characterized in two male gatherings as threatening, frightening and repulsive; a symbolically castrated hero who is afraid to let himself go in heterosexual love and runs away from his three women (which suggests, at the very least, a *fear* of impotence); and a doctrinaire appeal for homosexuality on a theoretical but not an actual basis. In the novel Aaron reaches a sexual dead end where he will not give himself to women and cannot submit himself to men. In the Bible, Moses' rod (the one which smote the rock in Horeb) was turned into a serpent by the angry Lord in Exodus 4:2-3 (Lilly alludes to this when he thinks: 'I *know* he'll bite me, like a warmed snake, the moment he recovers', 92); and in the novel, though male love is described as a blossoming rod or an eagle's wing, it is closer to another of Lawrence's favourite images: the snake with the tail in its mouth.

Aaron's Rod, which suggests but does not describe Aaron's final 'fathomless submission' to Lilly, is Lawrence's most radical, though still incomplete, commitment to male love. In *The Plumed Serpent*, Lawrence's theory of power is carried to extreme limits and finally results in Cipriano's total dominance and Kate's complete submission.

IV. THE PLUMED SERPENT

In the summer of 1923, just after Lawrence completed the first draft of *The Plumed Serpent*, rootlessness, isolation, poverty, illness, sexual problems and the tension of Mexico intensified his conflict with Frieda and produced the second and most severe crisis of his marriage. Mabel Luhan reports, with some satisfaction: 'I had heard that he and Frieda had gone to New York to sail for England, but that they had quarreled at the last moment and he had let her sail alone . . . She told me, long afterwards, that she thought they had come to a final separation'.[52] Lea agrees that Frieda arrived in England completely out of love with her husband; and Murry states: 'She had enough of Lawrence and his Mexican "moods", and in fact she had left him. She felt — rightly enough — no more loyalty to him.' Katherine Mansfield had died of tuberculosis in January and Lawrence was in America, so Frieda and Murry decided to travel to Germany together.

'On the journey', writes Murry:

> we declared our love to each other. She was sweet and lovely, altogether adorable, and she wanted us to stay together in Freiburg for a few days anyhow, and I wanted it terribly. The idea of our sleeping together, waking in each other's arms, seemed like heaven on earth. I was worn out with the long strain of Katherine's illness, and Frieda's love was a promise of renewal.

And Lawrence had been horrible to her in Mexico — something really had snapped between them. So I felt free to take Frieda, or thought I did; but when it came to the point, I didn't. . . . 'No, my darling, I mustn't let Lorenzo down — I can't.'[53]

Murry's loyalty seems rather insincere and unconvincing, for in his confusion of grief and love it is doubtful that the weak-willed Murry could have resisted the desires of the passionate and dominant aristocrat. Murry probably slept with Frieda but did not *take* her away from Lawrence. Tedlock, who edited Frieda's *Memoirs and Correspondence* (1961), states that whether Frieda's relationship with Murry before her separation from Lawrence 'was intimate or not is unclear; but that it became so now on her return to England is certain';[54] and Delavenay, Lawrence's most recent biographer, agrees with this judgment.[55] Their liaison led to the famous exchange at the Café Royal in 1923

when Lawrence, drunk and despairing, appealed to Murry not to 'betray' him: and he, drunk too but 'clairvoyant' spoke the celebrated words, 'I love you, Lorenzo, but I won't promise not to betray you.' They meant, as he [Murry] explained later on, 'I am full of affection for you and pity for what you are suffering; but I won't promise not to conceal my knowledge of why you are suffering.'[56]

Moore explains that 'it is now known that Murry meant he would not betray Lawrence with Frieda, who had proposed that she and Murry become lovers'.[57] But Tedlock is closest to the truth when he writes: 'Murry confessed rather vaguely to a betrayer's role, and thereby increased Lawrence's scorn . . . The failure of Murry's plan for a peaceful collaboration with Lawrence on *The Adelphi* no doubt reflects Lawrence's personal feelings over the affair with Frieda.'[58]

Murry's fourth wife, Mary, attempted to perpetuate the myth of Murry's loyal friendship with Lawrence when she told Lea how Frieda told Murry that 'Lawrence had always looked on him as his greatest friend; how deeply he had loved him, and that he had held John's last letter to him in his hand when he was dying'.[59] Lea dutifully records this improbable sentimental detail;[60] and he also reports that after Lawrence's death in February 1930, Murry 'sped to the south of France to pay his last respects to Lawrence. There, however, he met Frieda: and this time there was no holding back. "With her, for the first time in my life, I knew what fulfilment in love really meant." '[61] There is no trace of irony in Lea's account of Murry's 'last respects', nor any comment on Murry's morbid compulsion to sleep with Frieda after his wife's and her husband's deaths. The following year Murry performed the first sexual post-mortem on Lawrence in *Son of Woman.*

The effect of the Frieda-Murry affair on *The Plumed Serpent,* which Lawrence rewrote during 1924-5, was an intensification of Lawrence's wish for male friendship and his overwhelming need to dominate and even obliterate the sexual power of women. The novel deifies terror and slavery in sex. As Cipriano's atrocities increase, Kate's desires diminish: 'as the sex is exhausted, gradually, a keener desire, the desire for the touch of death follows on . . . [Then come] fatal wars and revolutions which really create nothing at all, but destroy, and leave emptiness.'[62]

By renouncing her sexual identity and becoming a kind of sexual cipher, 'the harem type' like Carlota and Teresa, whom she affects to despise but really resembles, Kate is no longer an alternative to homosexual love, as in the earlier novels — she is a stimulant or catalyst: 'It seemed to Kate that the highest thing this country might produce would be some powerful relationship of man to man. Marriage itself would always be a casual thing . . . Men and women should know that they cannot, absolutely, meet on earth.'[63] Ramón and Cipriano are more attracted to each other because both are attracted to Kate. Cipriano tells Kate, 'To me Ramón is *more* than life'; he worships her because she saved Ramón's life, and wants her to be a goddess in the Aztec pantheon in order to please Ramón.

The novel charts 'the death of her individual self', the degeneration of Kate from a woman who is revolted by the cruelty of the bullfight to one who is indifferent to Cipriano's bloody executions; from the wife of Joachim Leslie who '*can* only love a man who is fighting to *change* the world, to make it freer, more alive' (77), to one who marries Cipriano, a 'sinister to her, almost repellent' general who suppresses rebellions to preserve the interests of the conservative landowners; from 'a modern woman and a woman in her own right' who states, 'I'm not going to submit . . . Why should one give in', to one who believes that 'Without Cipriano to touch me and limit me and submerge my will, I shall become a horrible, elderly female. I ought to *want* to be limited. I ought to be *glad* if a man will limit me with a strong will' (457). By the end of the book Kate has learned what Lettie, Hermione, Gudrun, Lottie, Josephine, Tanny, the Marchesa and even Ursula have failed to learn, but her ideas are *donnée* and unconvincing, and what Lawrence intends to be her sexual apotheosis is merely her sexual degradation.

To Kate, Cipriano, whose name suggests venereal licentiousness, represents Ramón's definition of a man, 'a.column of blood, with a voice in it', a kind of eloquent penis. He is 'The mystery of the primeval world! She could feel it now in all its shadowy, furious magnificence. She knew now what was the black, glinting look in Cipriano's eyes' (324); and like Gudrun and Loerke who admire grotesque Aztec art, Kate and Cipriano 'kindled themselves at the subtle lust of the . . . Mexicans'.[64] Their sexual relationship is described in the metaphor of blood, which links it to the two dramatic climaxes of the novel: Ramón's oily rubbing of Cipriano's erect loins and secret places, and Cipriano's stabbing the hearts of the three blindfolded assassins. These rituals combine perversity and atrocity, just as in the *corrida* when the bull works his horns up and down inside the horse's belly 'with a sort of vague satisfaction', and in the murder and mutilation of the *hacienda* manager, whose penis is stuffed into his mouth.

The ritualistic rubdown represents 'the renewal of the old, terrible bond of the blood-unison of man, which made blood-sacrifice so potent a factor of life. The blood of the individual is given back to the great blood-being, the god, the nation, the tribe' (434). The ritual is introduced by Cipriano stabbing a 'treacherous cur' in the heart (a sort of wet-run for the later bloodbath); and it takes place, as in the three earlier novels, at a moment of sexual frustration for both men: when Kate refuses to live with Cipriano and returns to her house in Sayula, and when Ramón is tormented by the pious and moribund Carlota.

> Ramón came quickly to him, placed one of his hands over Cipriano's eyes, closing them. Ramón stood behind Cipriano, who remained motionless in the warm dark, his consciousness reeling in strange concentric waves, towards a centre where it suddenly plunges into the bottomless deeps, like sleep . . .
> And Cipriano began to feel as if his mind, his head were

melting away in the darkness; like a pearl in black wine, the other circle of sleep began to swing, vast. And he was a man without a head, moving like a dark wind over the face of the dark waters . .

Ramón bound him fast round the middle, then, pressing his head against the hip, folded the arms round Cipriano's loins, closing with his hands the secret places . . .

The last circle was sweeping round, and the breath upon the waters was sinking into the waters, there was no more utterance. Ramón kneeled with pressed head and arms and hands, for some moments still. Then he bound the loins, binding the wrists to the hips . . .

And both men passed into perfect unconsciousness, Cipriano within the womb of undisturbed creation, Ramón in the death sleep. (383–5)

This passage, which exemplifies what T. E. Lawrence calls an 'effort to make the solar plexus talk English prose',[65] has the familiar, though heightened characteristics of Lawrence's homosexual scenes: the powerful rhythm and highly charged abstract language, the biblical allusion to the mysterious beginning of Genesis, the fondling (or masturbation) of the genitals, and the mindless, swooning, orgasmic finale.

The execution, which immediately follows the initiation ceremony, is a savage regression to the elaborate ritual of death when 'the Aztecs raised their deity to heights of horror and vindictiveness' (64), and to Cipriano's quick movements as if flashing a knife into some helpless adversary: 'the clutching throb of [sexual] gratification as the knife strikes in and the blood spurts out!' (145). Cipriano's sanguinary execution unites him with the other Aztecs of the novel by allowing him to share the slaughter he missed during the attack on Ramón's house, when Kate shot and Ramón stabbed and the blood ejaculated out 'like a red projectile . . . [in] one final terrible convulsion from the loins of the stricken man' (309).

Though Kate has been married twice and has two children, Cipriano wants and wills her to be a virgin (a relic of the old religion):

His innermost flame was always virginal, it was always the first time. And it made her again always a virgin girl . . . So, when she thought of him and his soldiers, tales of swift cruelty she had heard of him: when she remembered his stabbing the three helpless peons, she thought: Why should I judge him? He is of the gods[66] . . . And every time he takes the flower of my virginity . . . it leaves me *insouciante* like a young girl. What do I care if he kills people? His flame is young and clean (409-10).

This symbolic virginal defloration, 'a mindless communion of the blood', links Kate with the blood sacrifice of the helpless peons. And her response to Cipriano's perverse *coitus interruptus* is also like a frightened virgin's reaction to the first experience of sex:

> By a dark and powerful instinct he drew away from her as soon as this desire rose again in her, for the white ecstasy of frictional satisfaction, the throes of Aphrodite of the foam. She could see that to him, it was repulsive. He just removed himself, dark and unchangeable, away from her . . . When this sort of 'satisfaction' was denied her, came the knowledge that she did not really want it, that it was really nauseous to her [that is, to *him*]. (439)

It is unbelievable that Kate would accept Cipriano's deliberate frustration of her sexual orgasm (which so intensified her love for Joachim), for his 'dark and powerful instinct' is actually a cruel desire to dominate her and make her submit to his will — the triumph of *unhealthy* authority, of power over love. The violent events of *The Plumed Serpent* are the *political* manifestation of Cipriano's struggle for sexual domination, and he suppresses the rebellions of peons as well as of Kate. Yet it is Cipriano's kind of power-hungry sex that Lawrence condemns when Connie Chatterley practises it before she meets Mellors: 'A woman could take a man without really giving herself away. Certainly she could take him without giving herself into his power. Rather she could use this sex thing to have power over him . . . She could prolong the connection and achieve her orgasm and her crisis while he was merely her tool.'[67] It is only when the *man* achieves this kind of sexual power and can dominate the woman at will that he loses his fear of woman and with it his need for homosexual love.

To escape from the unbearable conflicts he encountered in his relations with women, Lawrence evolved the theory, which he attempted to apply to Murry and Katherine Mansfield, that male love could be a way toward a higher form of marriage between man and woman. In all four novels the heroes experience failure with women and are drawn to homosexual love. Cyril has his moment of fulfilment, but then drifts away from George toward celibacy; Birkin's passion for Crich continues even after Gerald's death, and he replaces Gerald by anal intercourse with Ursula; Aaron never succeeds with women, and returns to Lilly at the end of the book; and Ramón renounces the pathetic Carlota and passes into 'perfect unconsciousness' with Cipriano.

Most of Lawrence's fiction either diagnoses the disease of heterosexual love or contains a powerful element of imaginary gratification. Lawrence portrays the failure of passionate love between Siegmund and Helena in *The Trespasser*, Paul and Miriam in *Sons and Lovers*, and Ursula and Skrebensky in *The Rainbow*. And in his stories 'The Fox', 'The Princess', 'The Virgin and the Gipsy' and 'St Mawr' and novels like *The Lost Girl* there is a recurrent Laurentian theme of a virile and passionate man of the people who ravishes, against her conscious will but with her subconscious acquiescence, a beautiful, sensitive and often aristocratic woman.

The idea of male dominance is also accepted by the heroines who are the main characters of Lawrence's last two novels, for in *The Plumed Serpent* Kate renounces her orgasm to satisfy Cipriano's 'column of blood'. And in *Lady Chatterley's Lover*, written during the last stage of tuberculosis, when he was impotent[68] and his sexual combats with Frieda had subsided into a calm resolution, Lawrence expresses a new 'adjustment of consciousness', a reciprocal tenderness and love. But Connie earns her passionate fulfilment only by submitting to male authority and, like Ursula, achieves her sexual apotheosis with the potent Mellors in anal intercourse. Though Lawrence is usually associated with the triumphant expression of heterosexual love, this love depends on male dominance and is seriously qualified by an ambivalent longing for homosexuality.[69]

BIBLIOGRAPHY

I. SOCIOLOGICAL AND CLINICAL

Allen, Clifford. *Homosexuality: Its Nature, Causation and Treatment.* London, 1958.
Allen, Clifford. *A Textbook of Psychosexual Disorders.* London, 1969.
Altman, Dennis. *Homosexuality: Oppression and Liberation.* London, 1974.
Bailey, Derek. *Homosexuality and the Western Christian Tradition.* London, 1955.
Berg, Charles and Clifford Allen. *The Problem of Homosexuality.* New York, 1958.
Berg, Charles and Aron Krich, eds. *Homosexuality: A Subjective and Objective Investigation.* London, 1958.
Bergler, Edmund. *One Thousand Homosexuals.* London, 1961.
Bieber, Irving. *Homosexuality: A Psychoanalytic Study.* New York, 1962.
Churchill, Wainwright. *Homosexual Behavior Among Males.* New York, 1968.
Cory, D. W. *The Homosexual in America.* New York, 1951.
Cory, D. W. and J. P. LeRoy. *The Homosexual and His Society.* New York, 1963.
Ellis, Havelock. *Sexual Inversion.* London, 1897.
Freud, Sigmund. 'Character and Anal Eroticism' and 'On the Transformation of Instincts, with Special Reference to Anal Eroticism'. *Collected Papers,* trans. Joan Riviere. London, 1950. II. 45–50, 164–71.
Freud, Sigmund. *Three Contributions to the Theory of Sex* (1905). New York, 1948.
Freud, Sigmund. *Three Essays on the Theory of Sexuality.* London, 1905.
Hauser, Richard. *The Homosexual Society.* London, 1962.
Humphreys, Laud. *Tearoom Trade: A Study of Homosexual Encounters in Public Places.* London, 1970.
Hyde, H. Montgomery. *The Other Love: A History and Contemporary Survey of Homosexuality in Britain.* London, 1970.
Karlen, Arno. *Sexuality and Homosexuality.* London, 1971.
Krafft-Ebing, Richard. *Psychopathia Sexualis.* London, 1899.
Magee, Bryan. *One in Twenty: A Study of Homosexuality in Men and Women.* New York, 1966.
Marmor, Judd, ed. *Sexual Inversion.* New York, 1965.
Pearsall, Ronald. *The Worm in the Bud: The World of Victorian Sexuality.* London: Pelican, 1971.
Rees, John and Harley Usill, eds. *They Stand Apart.* London, 1955.
Ruitenbeek, Hendrick, ed. *Homosexuality and Creative Genius.* New York, 1967.
Schofield, Michael. *Sociological Aspects of Homosexuality.* London, 1965.

Socarides, Charles. *The Overt Homosexual.* London, 1968.
Vidal, Gore. 'Sex and the Law' (1965). *Collected Essays.* London, 1974. Pp. 186-96.
Weinberg, Martin and Colin Williams. *Male Homosexuals.* London, 1974.
West, D. J. *Homosexuality.* London: Pelican, 1960.
Westwood, Gordon. *A Minority: A Report on the Life of the Male Homosexual in Great Britain.* London, 1960.
Wolfenden, Sir John. *Report of the Committee on Homosexual Offences and Prostitution.* London, 1957.

II. Biographical and Critical

Ackerley, J. R. *Hindoo Holiday.* London, 1932.
Ackerley, J. R. *Letters,* ed. Neville Braybrooke. London, 1975.
Ackerley, J. R. *My Dog Tulip.* London, 1956.
Ackerley, J. R. *My Father and Myself.* London, 1968.
Auden, W. H. *Forewords and Afterwords.* London, 1973.
Baldwin, James. 'The Male Prison'. *Nobody Knows My Name.* London, 1964. Pp. 130-5.
Brittain, Vera. *Radclyffe Hall: A Case of Obscenity?* London, 1968.
Buchen, Irving, ed. *The Perverse Imagination: Sexuality and Literary Culture.* New York, 1970.
Carpenter, Edward. *Homogenic Love.* Manchester, 1894.
Carpenter, Edward. *The Intermediate Sex* (1908). London, 1916.
Carpenter, Edward. *Love's Coming of Age.* London, 1896.
Carpenter, Edward. *My Days and Dreams.* London, 1916.
'The Homosexual Imagination'. *College English,* xxxvi (November 1974), 272-404 (special issue).
Croft-Cooke, Rupert. *Feasting With Panthers.* London, 1967.
Croft-Cooke, Rupert. *The Verdict of You All.* London, 1955.
Davidson, Michael. *The World, the Flesh and Myself.* London, 1962.
Delavenay, Emile. *D. H. Lawrence and Edward Carpenter: A Study in Edwardian Transition.* London, 1971.
DeMott, Benjamin. 'But He's A Homosexual . . .' *Supergrow.* New York, 1969. Pp. 17-34.
Dickinson, Goldsworthy Lowes. *Autobiography.* ed. Dennis Proctor. London, 1973.
Dickinson, Goldsworthy Lowes. *The Greek Way of Life.* London, 1898.
Eglinton, J. Z. *Greek Love.* New York, 1964.
Fiedler, Leslie. *Love and Death in the American Novel.* New York, 1966.
Gide, André. *Corydon* (1911). New York, 1950.
Gide, André. *Fruits of the Earth* (1897). London: Penguin, 1972.
Gide, André. *Oscar Wilde: A Study.* ed. Stuart Mason, Oxford, 1905.
Grosskurth, Phyllis. 'The Problem'. *John Addington Symonds: A Biography.* London, 1964. Pp. 262-94.
Hoffman, Stanton. 'The Cities of Night: John Rechy's *City of Night* and the

American Literature of Homosexuality', *Chicago Review,* xvii (1964), 195-206.

Holroyd, Michael. *Lytton Strachey.* 2 vols. London, 1967.

Hyde, H. Montgomery, ed. *The Trials of Oscar Wilde.* London, 1960.

Isherwood, Christopher. *Lions and Shadows.* London, 1938.

James, Clive. 'Auden's Achievement', *Commentary,* lvi (December 1973), 53-8.

Kaplan, David. 'Homosexuality and the American Theater: A Psychoanalytic Commentary', *Tulane Drama Review,* ix (1965), 25-55.

Leduc, Violette. *La Bâtarde.* London, 1965.

Mailer, Norman. 'The Homosexual Villain', *One,* iii (1955), 8-12.

Marcus, Steven. *The Other Victorians.* New York, 1966.

Maugham, Robin. *Escape From the Shadows.* London, 1972.

Morris, Jan. *Conundrum.* London, 1974.

Morris, John. *Hired to Kill.* London, 1960.

Nichols, Beverley. *A Case of Human Bondage.* London, 1967.

Norton, Rictor, 'The Homosexual Literary Tradition: Course Outline and Objectives.' *College English,* xxxv (March 1974), 674-92.

Reade, Brian, ed. *Sexual Heretics.* London, 1970.

Smith, Timothy D'Arch. *Love in Earnest.* London, 1970.

Sutherland, Alistair and Patrick Anderson, eds. *Eros: An Anthology of Male Friendship.* London, 1961.

Symonds, John Addington. *A Problem in Modern Ethics.* London, 1896.

Wilde, Oscar. *De Profundis.* London, 1949.

Wildeblood, Peter. *Against the Law.* London, 1955.

Worseley, T. C. *Flannelled Fool: A Slice of Life in the Thirties.* London, 1969.

NOTES

I. INTRODUCTION

1. Apart from Wilde, Gide, Proust, Forster and T. E. Lawrence, and the dubious cases of Tennyson, Flaubert, Hopkins and Huysmans, a list of the most important homosexual writers of the last hundred years would include (apart from living writers): Edward FitzGerald, Edward Lear, Walt Whitman, Swinburne, Walter Pater, Verlaine, Rimbaud, A. E. Housman, Frederick Rolfe, C. P. Cavafy, Lionel Johnson, Stefan George, Norman Douglas, Somerset Maugham, Gertrude Stein, Lytton Strachey, Virginia Woolf, Ronald Firbank, Siegfried Sassoon, Katherine Mansfield, Jean Cocteau, Vita Sackville-West, J. R. Ackerley, Henry de Montherlant, Garcia Lorca, Hart Crane, William Plomer, W. H. Auden and Yukio Mishima.

2. A survey could include Beckford's *Vathek* (1786), Balzac's *Lost Illusions* (1837-43), Huysmans' *Against Nature* (1884), Melville's *Billy Budd* (1891, published in 1924), and Hesse's *Narziss and Goldmund* (1930) as well as Hanley's *Boy* (1931), Angus Wilson's *Hemlock and After* (1952), Baldwin's *Giovanni's Room* (1956), Ackerley's *We Think the World of You* (1960) and Isherwood's *A Single Man* (1964).

3. The best lesbian stories are Balzac's 'The Girl With the Golden Eyes' (1834) and D. H. Lawrence's 'The Fox' (1922).

4. See also Deuteronomy 23:17, I Kings 14:24 and Jude 7 for condemnation of the abominations of the Sodomites and their 'going after strange flesh'.

5. Tobias Smollett, *Roderick Random* (New York: Signet, 1964), p. 339.

6. Gordon Rattray Taylor, *The Angel-Makers* (London, 1958), p. 78.

7. John Addington Symonds, *A Problem in Modern Ethics* (London, 1896), p. 135.

8. H. Montgomery Hyde, ed., *The Trials of Oscar Wilde* (London, 1960), p. 17 n4. Yet Wilde's syphilis did not prevent him from having sexual relations with Lord Alfred Douglas and many other men.

9. Ibid., p. 193.

10. Ibid., p. 371.

11. Ibid., p. 236. See Plato, *The Symposium*, trans. Walter Hamilton (London: Penguin, 1973), p. 83: 'The object of love is in all truth beautiful and delicate and perfect and worthy to be thought happy, but what feels love has a totally different character'. The opening phrase of Wilde's speech comes from 'Two Loves', a sonnet by Lord Alfred Douglas.

12. Hyde, p. 339.

13. Quoted in ibid., p. 12.

14. Ibid., pp. 128, 132. Stuart Mason, *Oscar Wilde: Art and Morality*, 2nd edn (London, 1912), pp. 231-57, lists the deletions from the serialized version. See also Isobel Murray, ed., *The Picture of Dorian Gray* (London, 1974).

15. Frank Harris, *Oscar Wilde: His Life and Confessions* (1916) (London, 1938), p. 171.

16. See Sir John Wolfenden, *Report of the Committee on Homosexual Offences and Prostitution* (London, 1957), pp. 149-51, for a summary of the law relating to homosexual offences in European countries.

17. J. R. Ackerley, *Letters*, ed. Neville Braybrooke (London, 1975), pp. 53-4.

18. Marcel Proust, *Cities of the Plain*, trans. C. K. Scott Moncrieff, ii (London: Chatto & Windus, 1971), 129.

19. See my essay, ' "To Die For Ireland": The Character and Career of Sir Roger Casement', *London Magazine*, xiii (April–May 1973), 23–50.
20. See Vera Brittain, *Radclyffe Hall: A Case of Obscenity?* (London, 1968).
21. Ackerley, *Letters*, p. 62.
22. Wolfenden, p. 25.
23. Irving Bieber, *Homosexuality: A Psychoanalytic Study* (New York, 1962), pp. 303–4.
24. See Lewis Moorman, *Tuberculosis and Genius* (Chicago, 1940) and Hendrik Ruitenbeek, ed., *Homosexuality and Creative Genius* (New York, 1967).
25. Friedrich Nietzsche, '*Thus Spake Zarathustra*', *The Portable Nietzsche*, trans. and ed. Walter Kaufmann (New York: Viking, 1954), p. 129.
26. Oscar Wilde, *Letters*, ed. Rupert Hart-Davis (London, 1962), p. 768 (6 December 1898).
27. Edward Sackville-West, 'A Modern Isaiah', *New Statesman*, xxvii (10 July 1926), 360.
28. Plato, '*Symposium*', *The Dialogues*, trans. Benjamin Jowett, i (Oxford, 1892), 548, and '*Phaedrus*', ibid., i.460.
29. E. M. Forster, *Maurice* (London, 1971), pp. 61–2.
30. W. T. Stead, 'The Conviction of Oscar Wilde', *Review of Reviews*, xi (June 1895), 492.
31. W. H. Auden, 'A Worcestershire Lad', *Forewords and Afterwords* (London, 1973), p. 327.
32. Proust, *Cities of the Plain*, i.41–2.
33. Brian Reade, 'Introduction' to *Sexual Heretics* (London, 1970), p. 53.
34. See Emile Delavaney, *D. H. Lawrence and Edward Carpenter: A Study in Edwardian Transition* (London, 1971).
35. Edward Carpenter, *Homogenic Love* (Manchester, 1894), p. 46.
36. André Gide, *Oscar Wilde: A Study*, ed. Stuart Mason (Oxford, 1905), pp. 49–51.
37. J. R. Ackerley, *E. M. Forster: A Portrait* (London, 1970), p. 19.
38. Thomas Mann, 'Introduction' (1951) to Albert Guerard, *André Gide*, 2nd edn (Cambridge, Mass., 1969), p. xxii.
39. Ibid., p. xxiv.
40. D. H. Lawrence, 'German Books: Thomas Mann', *Phoenix* (London, 1936), p. 312.
41. André Gide, *Journals*, trans. Justin O'Brien, i (London, 1948), 258 (April 1910).
42. Ibid., ii.265 (14 May 1921).
43. Marcel Proust, *Time Regained*, trans. Stephen Hudson (London: Chatto & Windus, 1960), p. 166.
44. Gide, *Journals*, ii.267 (May 1921).
45. E. M. Forster, 'Proust', *Abinger Harvest* (London, 1961), p. 117.
46. Quoted in Oliver Stallybrass, 'Introduction' to *The Life to Come* (London, 1972), p. xiv.
47. D. H. Lawrence, *Collected Letters*, ed. Harry Moore (London, 1962), pp. 316, 318, 323 (to Bertrand Russell and Mary Cannan).
48. See my essay, 'E. M. Forster and T. E. Lawrence: A Friendship', *South Atlantic Quarterly*, lxix (Spring 1970), 205–16.
49. *Letters of T. E. Lawrence*, ed. David Garnett (London, 1938), p. 537.
50. C. D. [T. E. Lawrence], 'D. H. Lawrence's Novels', *Spectator*, cxxxix (6 August 1927), 223.
51. E. M. Forster, 'Mr D. H. Lawrence and Lord Brentford', *Nation and Atheneum*, xlvi (11 January 1930), 509.
52. E. M. Forster, Letter to *Nation and Atheneum*, xlvi (29 March 1930), 888. D. H.